The Persuasion, Influencing & Sales Recipe, For Recruitment & Search Firm Owners

Terry Edwards

The Persuasion, Influencing & Sales Recipe For Recruitment & Search Firm Owners

Copyright © 2015 Terry Edwards

www.drewcoaching.com

First published in Great Britain in 2015 by Compass Publishing

ISBN 978-1-907308-52-9

Set by The Book Refinery Ltd

Printed and bound in the UK by Berforts Information Press.

Testimonials

 *"Happy to say that I have won business from putting Terry's methods into practice so I have no hesitation in recommending him to non-competitors especially if they are in a different geographical location!"*

Richard Blann
RandKA Flexible Recruitment Solutions

"Terry has an engaging style and a unique outside-the-box approach to recruiting methodologies which I appreciate. Continually being open to new ideas, communication styles  *and techniques related to our business is important given the ever-changing climate of the business environment."*

Joe S. Murawski
Focused Hire

 *I have been recruiting for nearly 10 years. When I was first approached by Terry Edwards I must confess I just couldn't imagine that you could get recruitment business without cold calling. You see, in all my recruiting career 'cold calling' and 'word of mouth' was the only way I was able to get business. That has all changed since working with Terry. There are two main benefits our business have got from working with Terry. The first one is, it has opened my eyes to the other effective methods of getting more clients. And secondly, in one week alone we generated 40 sales leads without making a single cold call. If you are serious about growing your recruitment business, I would recommend Terry Edwards."*

Jim Foster
Antal international Network

"If not for your insight and
inspiration I would not have had the
courage and motivation to make the
changes I have to improve my
marketing and business strategies.
We have changed our website to have a call to
action, have a proactive marketing strategy that is
consistent and producing results, numerous clips on
you tube that talk about who we are, a vision about
recruiting that allows us to stay true to who we are,
we don't need to be everything to every client we
just need to be the best at who we are. You are not
always right but dead on more than any other
recruitment coach and advisor I have found in 20
years."

Jeff Abram
SearchWest Inc.

 *"I have owned my own recruitment firm for 14 years now, and I must say I was reluctant to engage drewcoaching as I questioned if I would get my monies worth, also I believed that if there is anything that needs doing to improve the performance of the business then I would do it. However what I have found with working with drewcoaching is, I am more focused than at any other time in my career, it is also great to have a sounding board to vent some of my frustration that comes with running a recruitment business. The main advantage of engaging drewcoaching is my marketing knowledge has increased substantially and our sales have improved dramatically. If you are looking to increase sales and performance of your team I would recommend drewcoaching..."*

Eloise Shelton
Vanilla Recruitment

"I've been in business for over 17 years. Out of everything Terry has shared with me, I found the "permission marketing" aspects most useful.terry shared with me the attraction marketing process that encourages my potential clients to come to me, rather than me always having to chase them. I would recommend Terry to any Recruitment/Search Firm Owner who wanted to know more about marketing and attracting clients."

Curtis Baer
Barrington Search Group

"Terry has provided me with some very thought provoking comments and fresh ideas. Happy to recommend Terry's marketing advice and tips to other Recruitment Business owners who want more ideas around attracting clients."

Max Roberts
Walbrook Search

"We have been in business for 12 years. We specialize in placing marketing/digital marketing candidates in luxury categories including beauty and wine & spirits. Terry has provided me with some very helpful tips on attracting clients and increasing profits. I would definitely refer Terry to another recruiting firm who wanted to grow their business."

Jan Liscio
Patrickson-Hirsch Associates

"As a company, "Russells" have been in business for nine years. However, I worked for two other companies previously and have been around the Recruitment Industry for over 25 years. Terry seems to know exactly how difficult our market place is and knows all the pitfalls we come across on a day to day basis. In an industry notorious for it's secrecy, it's good to hear from someone who knows how you feel. We would be delighted to endorse Terry wherever we can."

Marge Russell
Russell Recruitment

"We've just finished our year end and have exceeded our STRETCHED target. (We beat our original target by 24% and our stretched target by 3%). Additionally we have raised the  *proportion of retained business from virtually nothing to about 50%, we have changed the structure of the business and have Business Development Consultants and Delivery Consultants (Resourcers) which makes us more effective. And finally (you will be proud of me), we are doing our first LIVE seminar at the NEC, to existing, old and potential new customers."*

Jon Salt
Affinity Search

 *"Terry, your clear step by step plans for generating leads, regardless of the delivery method is the number 1 most useful thing I am learning from you. Creative information that forces me to re-think business. It lifts the horse blinders in a sense!*

Your ability to connect with top performers and outline their successful processes is useful and it's great to be reminded to 'take action'...

Content generation is useful, and other lessons on how to appeal to our client base. I believe the "profit club" will be a useful addition as a gathering place for your materials that can be accessed anytime by your customers. I would certainly recommend you to non-competing firms."

Dave Drohan
Bridge Point Search

"I have been a recruitment business owner for 16 years and although I recognised the value of coaching I had a number of reservations about working with drewcoaching. I was  *concerned that as they are UK based and I am in Ireland, they may not be in touch with the economic and business nuances here. I also had reservations about the time I would need to commit with an already very busy work life. I have been working with drewcoaching for 6 months now and none of my initial reservations have held true. I am really enjoying the coaching process and the value it is bringing to my business. It's great to have an independent person who is interested and invested in the success of my business and who really understands the strategies, methods and techniques they are sharing with me as they have real business experience with them. It has also been reassuring to know that I am not going 'mad' on occasion and that my challenges are all fixable and changeable. I have been given the steps to take action and implement the changes needed to succeed. Even when the necessary changes have been quite difficult, drewcoaching have provided support and insight, which has increased my confidence in the actions across many aspects of managing my business. The practical aspect of their*

coaching around systems and process has been invaluable. Over the past six weeks since beginning to implement some of the structure and procedures into some areas of our recruitment process that were proving particularly challenging, we have had a great month in terms of revenue, which I directly attribute to the recent work I have been doing with drewcoaching. I wouldn't hesitate to recommend drewcoaching to any recruitment business not in competition with me. For any business that is, I would rather keep them a secret.."

Mark Markey
The Recruitment Bureau

"I have been a recruitment business owner for 15 years and in that time I have met numerous coaches and trainers. I wasn't keen at first to work with drewcoaching as I thought after nearly 15 years in the business there was little else I could learn about building a recruitment business, another concern was the fact I would be sharing my companies details with someone who works with many of my competitors Since working with drewcoaching, I have experienced an amazing transformation in business development. As a business we are able to generate more sales enquiries than ever in the history of the business and all of them without ever making a cold call. In fact we generated 82 leads in 4 days and signed one retained assignment, which when you consider we don't really sell retained recruitment that was quite an achievement, the marketing has been so successful that potential clients are calling us, we have had to put the marketing on stop as we are unable to cope with so many leads in a short period of time. If you are tired of cold calling and would like to discover how to have your clients calling you I would recommend drewcoaching."

Steve Hauge
Foundation Resourcing

 *"I appointed Terry in October 2010 as my Business Coach and since that day I have never looked back. He has been motivating in both my business life and at home.* He has helped me find the focus I needed to see through all the everyday 'firefighting' that can 'cloud' your judgement and made me realise that by taking responsibility for your actions and in-actions everyday, you will achieve your goals. 'Goals' is also another watch word with Terry, without them there is no destination and whilst anyone can set goals, Terry will enable you to exceed them in every way. In addition to the weekly coaching sessions, he is always available to provide guidance at the end of the phone. His knowledge of marketing, his reason to be and the value of time has made a significant difference to the results I am seeing in my business. Terry you are an inspiration and a star."*

Melanie Bose
Omnium IT Recruitment Limited

"I find the marketing tips and information Terry shares interesting and really get a lot of value and benefit from them, I have often forwarded them on to others and  *just find them a good read. Not too much information and not too long and "waffling" I find that I feel like I know who you are, really enjoy your writing. I would be happy to recommend Terry to other Recruitment/Search Firms... I work closely with a number of other recruiters and search firms, I find that in this economy we need to and benefit from working together. I do a number of splits with other agencies, I think we need to change how we see and do things, I have been so grateful to be able to get help and to give help to other colleagues, I think we all need to get an "abundance" mentality... lets all work together and share... a half a loaf of bread is far better than no bread at all."*

Debra Manson
Debra Manson Recruitment & Training

 *"I have only been working with Terry for a few months but he has already transformed my thinking and the results are now there to see. He has a clear understanding of what needs to be done and has helped me to implement a client attraction system that works. I would happily recommend Terry to any non competitor of mine."*

Lee Hancock
i4C Executive Search Limited

Contents

Who Is This Book For?

You're a beginner in the recruitment/search industry as a business owner, and have done a couple of pitches and they have 'bombed'.

That's because you didn't have this foolproof blueprint which contains all the 'trial and errors' of selling recruitment/search that have created millions in revenue for the top guys. These people know what sells and the psychology behind it—and I know for sure that *'The Persuasion, Influencing and Sales Recipe For Recruitment & Search Firm Owners'* will help you get the business the next time you go into that meeting.

You're a Recruitment/Search owner with a team, and you have been in the business for years. You and your team are looking for some more 'tricks' you can use to boost your profits.

You are an owner of a Recruitment/Search business, and you do most of the billings for the team. In fact, you are working to pay the wages of the under performers in your team, and you would like your team to be billing at the same level as you, and doing it consistently.

The good news is that all of your prayers will be answered in this book - which contains *just about* every single psychological and practical tactic to ensure your next pitch for business sells and your clients come back to you again and again. That way you can create a scalable business with predictable income month after month, year after year.

Listen: to get the same 'know-how' that I have would take you YEARS of trial and error, spending hours… days… and MONTHS testing different approaches to selling recruitment/search to see what works.

Well guess what? I've already done all the hard work for you! Just follow the blueprint I share, and you could be just like the 'World's Top Performers' who sell with integrity, ease and comfort, and make a ton of money.

So I'm saving you essentially, *THOUSANDS of dollars/pounds* of time, heartache and beating your head against the wall. And if you value your time at all, this book is worth at least $10,000/£6,467 if you are solo recruiter, in the first month, and many times more if you have a team.

So if there is a gap in between where you are now and where you would like to be, read this book and discover what the top recruitment/search firm owners are doing, then you can do it too.

But first of all I have a confession to make. I have to be absolutely honest with you right from the start.

You see, before I share with you how you can increase your sales and your personal income, I have to lay some groundwork first.

Well when I say *"I"*, I'll be dragging *you* along for the ride as well. After all, it is your recruitment/search business.

So while I can hold your hand - to some degree - you've got to do the work *yourself.*

In other words, there is no point reading this book and thinking 'that was good'...

No, no, no!

You have to take **ACTION and implement what you are about to discover.**

It would be a bit like going to your local gym because you're fat, unhealthy and out of shape. You pay your monthly membership and you are full of enthusiasm and good intentions. In the first week, you go four times and reduce your calorie intake. The next week you get caught up in meetings and you're tired and hungry, so you have the odd beer and cheese burger with fries. *"Hell, a person has to eat, right?"* And you promise yourself that you *will* get back into it the next week. But of course, you don't and the consequences are; your still fat, unhealthy and out of shape.

Your friends ask how you're getting on. You explain that you have a slow metabolic rate and the gym is not working for you.

Do you know anyone who is like that? Is that someone you know really well? In fact, do you see them every time you look in the mirror?

There is a great quote that I often refer too, which goes, *"How you do anything, is how you do everything!"*

Now, you may well decide to be insulted by that. But just another word of warning, there is every chance you may decide to be insulted or offended by more of what you are about to discover in this book. You see, I have one intention and one intention only: **to help you make more money and work fewer hours,** *nothing more, nothing less.*

I am plain speaking and will not pull any punches. I am not

politically correct and have some opinions you may not share or like. So if you are in any way precious and don't like to be told how it is, then this book is not for you.

Please pay a lot of attention here: this book is not a panacea for all *recruitment/search business ills* and nor is it a magic pill.

Also, I wish I could take credit for what you are about to discover. The fact is, what you are about to discover comes from some of the most successful and very rich Recruitment and Search firms from around the world and from some of the greatest marketing and client attraction experts in the world. It also comes from some of the world's leading marketers and recruitment sales training gurus

This book will provide you with enough fuel to get your motor running and to get you started. It will provide you with the necessary information to formulate a solid action plan and should you implement it, you will see real results.

One of the top marketing experts is Dan Kennedy - if you haven't already, you should become familiar with his work immediately!

His material single-handedly changed how I view sales & marketing, and any success I've personally had I attribute directly to him and many like him.

In one of his brilliant no BS books, he talks about how the majority of business owners lack any sort of core ambition.

He states:

"In whatever population it is you are selling or marketing to, there are surprisingly few genuinely ambitious people. Now they speak ambition, so if you ask them they will say things that would make you think they are ambitious. They do that because they know they're

supposed to. If you put them in a focus group and do research with them, they will say the right things to indicate they are ambitious. But their behaviour tells a different story."

What he says is important in the context of the information I will reveal to you in this book. Remember what I said earlier, *"How you do anything, is how you do everything!"*

If, during the course of reading through the nuggets, you find yourself thinking things like, *"That sounds like too much work"* or, *"Ah, I wouldn't be able to do that"* - or perhaps, *"But my market is different..."* then the game is up for you!

It means you've resigned yourself to being one of those people who merely talks ambition. Now there's nothing wrong with this, but if you wish to join the other group, the group of business owners who are ambitious, you're going to have to take action - and lots of it.

There is no other way.

The top recruitment/search firms that have created multi-million pound firms KNOW what works and what doesn't when it comes to getting people to BUY Recruitment or Search. And it doesn't happen by accident. It all has to do with following a certain 'recipe' for selling Recruitment/Search services. And note, it is a *recipe*, not a menu. For this to work for you, ALL of the ingredients supplied in the book **must be applied!**

Introduction

It is estimated that there are over **200,000 search and recruitment firms** in English speaking countries.

The average hiring manager gets between 5-20 cold calls a day, every day, from recruiters and search firms all claiming to be good recruiters.

Yep! The average hiring managers get as many as 400 cold calls a month from recruiters, so you are in an extremely competitive market, and most of you will not be around in five years' time if you keep doing what you are doing now.

According to recent research, between 70-80% of search and recruitment firms FAIL in the first five years. And of those that remain, about 5% are just getting by. And there is a reason for that. Most hiring managers have NO RESPECT for you or what you do. Think about it. How many prospects knock you back on your fees, ask you to send your terms and tell you they will get back to you? They rarely - if ever - do.

How many hiring managers insist that you only get paid on results? In other words, you do the work and you might get paid for it. Hell, even a prostitute gets paid upfront. The implication of this is that many recruitment and search firm owners lie in bed at 2am in a cold sweat, wondering if they'll make payroll or targets.

Yet on the other hand, the top billers know how many leads they are going to generate and how much more money they will make. This is because they have a tried and tested system for getting clients to buy from them.

In this book you will discover what the most successful recruiters in the world are doing, and what works when it comes to selling recruitment and search. So much so that prospects will want to buy from you more than you want to sell to them. When you apply these methods to your business you will reap the rewards of more business and increase your personal income.

And that's all there is to it.

Yet I will continue to hear the same old comments, such as, *"Yeah, but my business is different"* / *"My clients will not pay a retainer."* Or, *"I work in a market that is price driven."*

If you insist on holding on to that limiting thinking, it is worth asking yourself this question: *"How would I behave if I thought like the top billers who only work on retainers or exclusive, who never ever negotiate on price?"*

Look, if you offer a good recruitment/search service that more than meets your prospect's needs, then read on. If your service is not so good and you are not as competent a recruiter as your competitor, then this is not for you.

I've worked with some of the most successful recruitment/search firm owners in the world in my 27 years in the recruitment industry. I have witnessed guys starting from nothing and going on to create multi-million firms, in some cases in less than two years. These highly successful guys are masters at communication, influencing and persuasion. And that in itself is very important...

If you think these highly successful guys are smooth talking one hit wonders with the gift of the gab, you are so wrong.

"The fact is, selling recruitment/search services isn't about the gift of the gab, or being the cheapest, or even being the best provider of search or recruitment."

This is where many recruiters - including those doing OK - screw things up. They think they can just get on the phone and pester some hiring managers. Your prospects don't enjoy receiving cold calls and will do anything to get rid of the recruiter, including giving them job orders. You see, today's hiring managers are a lot more sophisticated; they have to be.

The most successful recruitment and search firm owners know there are a whole host of psychological triggers, that when used correctly in their presentation, not only boost their selling power and earnings, but also ensure your customers keep buying again and again.

Here's what you'll discover when you read this book:

- ✓ The personality traits of the top billers worldwide, some of these will certainly surprise you.

- ✓ The hidden and rarely revealed psychological triggers that can influence the client to want to pay you a higher fee.

- ✓ The little known secret that explains why your prospects will never ever buy from you, and what to do about it.

- ✓ Why your childhood has such a negative impact on your sales success, and what to do about it.

- ✓ How to get clients coming to you ready to buy.

✓ How to generate more leads than you can handle, and never ever make another cold call again.

✓ The 19 words to use at the beginning of every sales meeting to increase your conversions by 25%.

✓ Access to killer sales scripts that have resulted in your competitors making millions in fees.

One of my personal beliefs is, *"There is nothing wrong in not having any business, the only shame is not doing anything about it."*

I do think, however, that there is shame in being too stupid or cheap to invest in yourself by acquiring know-how.

Over the years, I have heard varied excuses from people as to why they are not enjoying the success of the few. The silly, *"But my recruitment business is different,"* is simply a confession lacking creative thinking.

The other one is time. Some recruiters rationalise that tomorrow will be a better time to begin to learn and improve, ignoring the fact that we live only in the present and that procrastination is the language of the poor.

The one thing about time is that it does not discriminate, regardless of your wealth, gender, sexual preferences, colour or religion. We all get the same amount of time. It's just that the top achievers use it better than the underperforming recruitment/search firm owners.

Part 1: What Is Selling Recruitment & Search?

"Selling recruitment/search is an exchange of recruitment services for money, nothing more, nothing less" ~ *Terry Edwards*

What is your perception of SELLING?

For many people when they are asked to describe a sales person, the image is not that flattering. Maybe some slick, smooth individual dressed in a certain way, who gets through life with the gift of the gab. To some people the image is of some slippery, slimy person who, quite frankly, is a bit dodgy and cannot be trusted.

But wait a minute; take a look at your average day...

This for me is a typical day:

I have three children, two of whom are still at home. I spend most of my time trying to convince or persuade them to do something, or not do something.

I am a keen triathlete and there is a new stationary bike on the market called the Watts bike. This bike is the closest thing to a road bike and it measures wattage amongst other things. Oh, and it retails for about £2,500/$4,000. Now, I'm sure you can imagine the conversation I have with my wife about getting one. Her objections are, *"But you already have a stationary bike, a road bike and a mountain bike. Why on earth do you need to spend*

£2,500/$4,000 on another bike just so you can measure the wattage?"
This is an ongoing conversation/sales negotiation that I have
with my wife.

I then head off to the office and have to negotiate a parking
space with the receptionist, as there are only 50 parking spaces
for an office with 120 companies based in it. (I really don't
understand that!) I then have to convince a member of my
team to build a website for one of my clients in just 4 hours,
as they have a major launch and forgot to revamp their
website.

Every day, I receive emails and calls from potential prospects.
I have to convince them that I don't work with **any**
recruitment/search firms and that they have to qualify before
I will consider working with them.

I then meet a friend for lunch and have to persuade the waiter
to move us to another table as the table we are on is near the
front door and it is bitterly cold outside. Every time someone
enters the building we are exposed to minus 10C. The waiter
explains that they are fully booked and there are limited tables
available.

Then it is back to the office to convince my publisher that I
need more time to get this book completed.

I could go on, but I'm sure you get the point.

If you think about your typical day, I suspect it wouldn't be
much different from mine, in terms of influencing and
persuading people to do something.

There is of course the little matter of explaining to potential
prospects why they should engage you; why they should let
your firm work exclusively on the assignment; why they
should invest in a retainer; why they should see the candidates

you put forward and why selected candidates should take the job offer.

Of course, you may also have a team who you have to cajole, persuade or convince.

Call it what you like, there are many names for it such as:

⮑ Selling

⮑ Negotiating

⮑ Influencing

⮑ Convincing

⮑ Persuading

⮑ Business development

⮑ Closing the deal

⮑ Asking for the order

⮑ Communicating effectively

⮑ Vending

⮑ Bartering

⮑ Peddling

⮑ Trading

Whatever you call it, it has to be done. The harsh reality is, if you don't do it your competitors will, and they will get the business and the income and you will be broke.

In my experience of working with some of the top recruiters

in the world, the methods using the 'hard sell' are very short term. Sure, you may win a deal here and there, but they tend to be one off deals.

The 'hard sell' is so wrong and under no circumstances should you use those kinds of methods for getting more business. You see, the 'hard sell' tactic puts a great deal of psychological pressure on prospects to engage.

Cold calls: unsolicited sales pitches delivered with force; closing techniques that create high levels of urgency. These are there to do one thing - *sell something.* They know it, you know it, and everybody knows it. And very few people enjoy it. (I explain more about cold calls in Part 6.)

In fact, let me ask you a question: has a hiring manager ever said to you, *"I really enjoying having my time interrupted by endless cold calls from recruiters?"*

And what about you? How do you feel when you are at home with your family, about to sit down with them for your evening meal, when the phone rings? You rush over to answer it and get the dreaded sales pitch. Have you ever said to the sales person on the other end of the phone, *"Thank you so much for interrupting my precious time with my family to tell me about the great product you want to sell to me that I have no need for"?*

Of course not…

There are a lot of recruitment and search sales programmes out there, which are full of misinformation and tell you that this is how you get business for your firm.

If this is what you're expecting from this book, then you're sadly mistaken and will be disappointed. While it can be effective some of the time, even if you have the best recruitment service and the best candidates in the entire world, this tactic can turn off prospects, or worse, make you sound like every other recruiter out there. And believe me, it is not attractive.

Very few people enjoy being sold to; your prospects like to buy. Think about it, when you're in a store and the sales assistant says, *"Can I help you?"*, you're more likely to tell them that you are just looking. The last thing you want is to be sold to. So stop doing the 'hard sell'!

Yes, I appreciate that may seem counter intuitive, but bear with me.

Do what the top recruiters do

Our research shows that top billers continue to make 80% of the all the recruitment/search income and sell ten times more than their peers and competition, regardless of the economy. Knowing this alone doesn't do much good, but knowing why this happens is invaluable.

The sales tactics that once worked are no longer working.

Fortunately, the new methods for generating sales are skills that can be learned and mastered. Those that do will join the top 20% who are earning 80% of the money. Those that don't will reside in the land of struggle and uncertainty.

The economy is uncertain. In fact, the whole world is uncertain; plus, there are so many alternatives to using a recruiter, which means prospects are sitting on their wallets and doing everything they can to not spend money with you.

It's a very competitive market out there and many people are losing sales, even with a good offer, match of needs, right targets, budgetary fit, and so on. BUT, top billers don't seem to be affected by ANY of this.

So, to get the answer to the question - *"What have the top 20% done differently in order to earn 80% of the recruitment revenue over the last several years?"* - just read this book and implement what you are about to discover.

There is a gift waiting for you from the kind and extremely generous 'Renegade Recruiter'

Before you go any further, make sure you go to
www.recruitmentsalesrecipe.co.uk/inner-circle
and get the tools, templates and scripts which will enable
you to influence your prospects and candidates effortlessly
and with integrity, so that you can increase
your personal earnings.

This normally sells for £297.00/$465.00 but you can get it
FREE! Simply go to;
www.recruitmentsalesrecipe.co.uk/inner-circle

Part 2: Why Most Recruitment/Search Firms Fail & What To Do About It

Building a successful recruitment/search business is NOT as simple as getting on the phone and pestering prospects or being a great networker.

A deep understanding of the *'sales process'*, the important consumer psychology embedded in selling and the mindset of top billers is critical to creating a strong, sustainable, profitable business.

When you read this book and take ACTION, you'll get this 'secret recipe'. So, without further ado, let's get going and start putting some money in your back pocket, NOW!

The 3 different types of recruitment/search firms

It is argued that there are three different types of Recruitment/Search firms in the world, and those are;

Group A –These guys tend to be strong and ambitious. They are willing to sharpen their skills to improve performance.

Group B -These guys tend to be cynical of anything that is new and different. (They will say things like, *"We have always done it this way."*)

Group C – These are non-sales people, who don't like any form of selling and tend to be uncomfortable asking for business.

You may not like the idea of these three groups. You may think the list is unfair, you may even decide to be insulted. I suggest that there is not much point in forming any opinion until you have read this book.

Let me explain why…

Let's take a very quick and simplistic overview of the recruitment/search market and the problems you are facing, and believe me, you are facing some massive challenges.

"Only the select few are getting it right."

The sad fact is, most recruitment/search firms are getting it so wrong.

Let's look at the facts:

> ➢ 5% of recruitment/search business owners are very successful

> ➢ 15% are getting there

> ➢ 60% are getting by

> ➢ 20% are struggling

This explains why 20% of recruitment/search firms have 80% of the market.

The sad fact is that 80 out of every 100 recruitment/search firms go bust in the first five years of trading. Five years after that, of the 20 survivors, you'll have just four left. Then five years after that, you're down to one.

In other words, there's a 99% chance of you going out of business in the first 15 years of operation.

That's a very scary but true statistic, and the bad news for you if you've been in business 15 years or less as of today, and if you follow the crowd and do what 80% of recruitment/search firms do, is that you will be mediocre at best.

Does mediocrity appeal to you?

Would you like to be called a mediocre recruiter? A mediocre wife or husband? A mediocre friend? How would you feel if your children said you were a mediocre parent? What if your partner said you were a mediocre lover?

Well, unless you do something different to the majority of recruitment/search firms, that's exactly what you will be: *a mediocre recruiter, getting mediocre results.*

But it's not easy, by any stretch of the imagination.

The top reasons why you're struggling to get business

There are numerous challenges you are facing, such as:

Your direct competitors: It is estimated that in Australia, the United Kingdom and the USA, there are just over a million people claiming to be recruiters of one kind or another. In whatever town or city you are in, you will be aware of the competition you have, and that is only the start.

Your competition comes from all over the world: Technology has made the world smaller. That means you aren't just competing with companies that offer similar recruitment/search services in your town, but you could be competing with companies from across the world.

Alternatives to using YOU as recruiter: Freelance websites, such as www.elannce.com, have a very interesting system. There is the common set-up of prospects posting available jobs and then waiting for people to apply for them from all over the world.

In addition to jobs being posted by employers, the freelancers themselves can post their own proposals to sell themselves to potential prospects. One of the suggested ways of doing this is to create a 30 second video showcasing their skills. It's a great idea that helps to put the power back into the hands of freelancers to present themselves in the way they know best.

The job board: That's right – prospects doing the work themselves.

Search engines: Search engines such as Google, Yahoo and Bing are other effective sources for finding a job. All your prospects have to do is type in the title of the job and their city and state and a number of listings will pop up from different websites.

Job fairs: Most cities have several job fairs per year, and they are usually advertised in newspapers or online.

Networking: Networking is another excellent way to find a job without a recruiter.

Social networking: You can post your resume on social networking sites such as Facebook and LinkedIn. Facebook has its own Job Board (as of November 2012), which includes 1.7 million jobs from recruiting companies. Facebook reported that 54 percent of all employers use its Job Board to post openings. LinkedIn sets the standard for professionals who want to post their resumes for others to see, and helps them network via their connections.

The recruitment process outsourcing (RPO) industry: This industry generated £2.8bn in revenue in 2013, a figure that could increase by another £500m a year over the next two years. It is estimated that 75% of European and 62% of North American businesses either have RPO arrangements in place, or are likely to *'seriously explore'* doing so over the next two years, making the industry a very big deal.

Of the RPOs surveyed, 85% of the work focuses on external hires, with 15% involving internal hiring. The most purchased RPO service is candidate sourcing.

Then there are the alternatives to taking on new staff: Since recruitment can be expensive and time consuming, other options might be considered, including:

- Reorganising the company structure.

- Sharing out work among existing employees.

- Promoting existing staff.

- Asking part-time employees if they would consider full-time work or taking on some additional hours.

- Improving the efficiency of the business, perhaps by rearranging tasks or utilizing technology.

- Offering overtime.

- Adopting flexible working arrangements, e.g., allowing some staff to begin earlier/later to provide cover for a longer part of the day.

- Hiring temporary workers.

- Offering short-term graduate internships through Graduate Talent Pool or other schemes, such as the Graduate Acceleration Programme (GAP).

- Secondments.

- Apprenticeships .

What about the global economy?

The global economy is weaker than many experts had envisaged, even six months ago. Only a modest pickup is foreseen for 2017, as the outlook for potential growth has been pared down.

Prospects differ, of course, across countries and regions. In fact, this is one of the most striking characteristics of the current economic conjuncture: it is very country specific.

Among advanced economies, the rebound is expected to be strongest in the United States and the United Kingdom, modest in Japan and weakest in the euro area, within which there are disparities.

Emerging markets and developing economies have been doing much of the heavy lifting during this crisis, accounting for more than 80 per cent of world growth since 2008. Led by Asia, and China in particular, we expect that they will continue to help drive global activity. For them too, however, it is likely to be at a slower pace than before.

Your prospects have unbelievable access: All they have to do is whip out their smart phone to access information about your prices, service, reputation, as well as your competitors. You must not only be aware of this, but you must also adapt to it and avoid being a commodity.

There is a fear of spending: Companies are shy about spending. In this climate there is no room for sloppiness and average or below average recruitment sales people.

As you have probably realised, there are a many hurdles in the way of you getting recruitment/search business.

Not getting this right will have a profound and negative impact on YOU and YOUR family. As a recruiter, your financial success, the future of your family's security and your peace of mind depends on you and your team being able to get the best from your marketing activity, by turning those warm leads you get into fee paying prospects.

A couple of caveats when I say 'marketing activity': I'm not referring to pestering your prospects with 'cold calls'. I'm referring to what the top firms do and that is to have the prospect come to them, so they are a 'welcome guest'. There is a massive difference.

*And when I say 'selling', I don't mean when a prospect says, "Send me your terms and I will get back to you." / "If you have any good candidates let me know." Or, "here is a job order you can try and fill, but by the way you're competing with a ton of other recruiters". That is **not** selling recruitment. If you think it is, then you're either broke or soon will be!*

The recruitment and search firm owner fantasy: recruitment/search business owners have a fantasy, which goes something like this:

I will go off and start my own recruitment business, I will then recruit other top billing consultants to come and join me. I will get them billing and I will get very rich and impress my friends and family then live happily ever after, just like they do in the films.

That fantasy is as likely to happen as me getting a date with Halle Berry. Sure, I can dream about it, I can imagine what it would be like, and I know my friends would be impressed if it was ever to, but it isn't going happen!

Working smarter, not harder

In all the years I have been working with recruitment and search firms from around the world, I can honestly say that 99% of owners would like to increase their sales and personal income.

If I were to ask the question: *"Are you willing to work harder to achieve the success you desire?"* I will often get some mutterings in the room from delegates saying things like, *"I work an 80 hour week now, I cannot work any harder."*

The purpose of this book is all about *working smarter*, **not harder.**

> *"Do what successful recruiters do and you will get what successful recruiters have got"* ~ *Terrythecoach*

There is a gift waiting for you from the kind and extremely generous 'Renegade Recruiter'

Before you go any further, make sure you go to **www.recruitmentsalesrecipe.co.uk/inner-circle** and get the tools, templates and scripts which will enable you to influence your prospects and candidates effortlessly and with integrity, so that you can increase your personal earnings.

This normally sells for £297.00/$465.00 but you can get it **FREE!** Simply go to; **www.recruitmentsalesrecipe.co.uk/inner-circle**

Part 3: Whatever You Believe *Is* True

The Land of the Giants

One day, at the beginning of your life, giants populated the land. You found it quite terrifying, the noise in particular, which was something you had never experienced before.

After a short time you discovered that some of these giants really cared for you. And they would spend a lot of time with you, feeding you, washing you, soothing you when you were not well and changing your clothes.

A few years later, these same giants yelled at you for what seemed liked no reason whatsoever. You were petrified that the people who had previously cared for you now yelled at you. You felt you could never really trust these giants again until you learned the rules of survival.

You found that the more you adopted their beliefs and some of their behaviours, the safer you became.

The giants shared their beliefs about their religion with you.

The giants shared their beliefs with you about wealth, such as, "money is the root of all evil". You did not realise that this is a misquote. And imagine how you felt when the giants told you that "selling" was a bad profession and no one likes sales people.

When in fact, the whole worldwide economy could not survive without sales and commerce.

Sometimes the giants would question your intelligence, or even your beauty, and call you nasty names to undermine and control you. Plus it made them feel better themselves.

The giants would tell you what your potential was, and what you were going to achieve in life. And even if the giants' beliefs about you were negative and disempowering, you adopted all their beliefs as YOUR own.

A few years later you met other little people just like you, and although initially a bit uncomfortable, you began to feel more secure with these little people who liked what you liked and played the same games as you.

After a period of time, you began to work out what you needed to do in order to be safe and survive.

You were told by giants, in their booming God-like voices, "Do as you are told, it is easier to get along if you go along, don't cry, don't fight, study hard, get a job, get married. Have children to support you in old age, always do as you are told." This list of what you must do to survive goes on and on.

Your tiny body grows larger and eventually you realise that there are no giants left.

Then one day you wake up, and there is this tiny creature looking at you. This tiny creature has awakened in the land of giants. And because you love this tiny creature, you begin to teach it everything you have been taught by the giants to survive.

And so the cycle continues...

The message from this story is quite simple. As a child, adults told you many things. You had no reason to question what you were told. For you to survive as a child, you realised you had to behave in a certain way; if you didn't there would be problems. Your beliefs about what you deserve to have in life are often a reflection of what you were told. If your parents, siblings, or a person in authority constantly told you that you were never going to amount to much, then that is your belief. If they told you that you were capable of achieving everything that you desire, then that is your belief.

Whatever you believe is true to YOU

These beliefs govern our lives, emotions, health, skills and every experience you can think of. You can believe ANYTHING. Some people believe in witchcraft, some people believe that 9/11 was an inside job and some believe that terrorists committed the atrocious act. I once went to a wedding and there was a lady there wearing what looked like cycling shorts; I suspect she believed it was OK to wear cycling shorts to a wedding!

What did you believe as a child that you no longer believe as an adult? What about Santa? When did you realise that Santa doesn't exist? Do you perpetuate the myth of him? And how do you justify the lie that you tell children, if you repeat the same story about Santa?

Two people can experience exactly the same thing yet draw different conclusions from it based on their experience.

Recently, I had a mini family reunion with my four sisters. Although we all live relatively close to one another, it's rare that you'll get us all in one room at the same time, so it's always an experience, to say the least.

My sisters and I have all had the same upbringing, more or less. We are all different ages though, so I guess there could have been slight differences, but more or less, it would have been exactly the same.

My three youngest sisters have been successful in their respective fields, but for whatever reason, it seems to have shaped my eldest sister differently. Despite claiming that she doesn't want to be, she's jobless and has been for many years. Instead of taking responsibility for this, she believes that the government and anyone else she can think of is to blame for the fact that she's unemployed and doesn't have enough money.

Anyway, the subject of school came up, and for some reason, she seems to believe that the reason she's struggling in her current life is because she struggled at school, and the reason she struggled at school is because (she believes) the teachers were racist.

Let me be the first to point out that a person's school life has absolutely nothing to do with what they do or don't achieve in later life. You don't have to look far to see that's true, but the racist thing is a possibility I guess, except she seems to be overlooking the fact that her three sisters and her brother had the exact same teacher and got on just fine.

Crazy I know!

I bet you know people that have what is called 'disempowering beliefs', and instead of rolling up their sleeves and doing something about them, they moan about the cards they've been dealt.

It's no different to some of the tired excuses I hear from struggling recruitment/search firm owners, who don't have all the prospects they want, but instead of doing something about it, they believe that the only way to get business is to cold call. And because they believe that prospects pay on price and price alone, they offer the lowest fees, yet still don't get the business they want.

They believe that 'selling' recruitment is a dishonourable job. They will say things like, *"I don't want to be too salesy."* So they wait by their phones, waiting for the prospects to call them.

They believe that marketing will not work for them, as their business is different, even though their competitors and other professionals in their field seem to be getting on fine, despite all of the above.

My point is, the government, your 'racist' teacher, the economy...these things are just beliefs.

Beliefs become a self-fulfilling prophecy

And it means you will act accordingly:

➤ If you believe marketing doesn't work, you will not do it.

➤ If you believe that selling recruitment is dishonourable, then you will behave accordingly.

➤ If you believe that no one wants to buy from you, you will find evidence to support that and you will behave as such.

➤ If you believe that prospects buy on price and price alone, you will find those types of prospects.

➤ If you believe that prospects will never ever pay you a retainer, then you will never ask for a retainer.

So having negative and disempowering beliefs creates negative and disempowering results. And the opposite is also true. If you expect to pitch to the client, offering a retainer service at the standard fee, and you expect success, then it is more likely that you will get it.

Failure equals success for disempowering beliefs and success equals success for empowering beliefs.

Your beliefs also come from:

Your environment: For example, think of any religion and ask yourself these questions: What beliefs do I have about this religion?/Where did I get those opinions from?

Your education: For example, if you studied psychology at college, you may have beliefs about what YOU can achieve in life.

Previous events: Although the past doesn't equal the future, it can sometimes influence it. If someone complimented you on something you were wearing, your belief would be influenced to wear it again, due to the previous compliment

> *And whatever belief you have, you can find evidence to support that belief. Your attention can focus on anything it chooses to support.*

Our beliefs control how we live our lives, and if we choose to live our lives acting on our self-limiting beliefs, then we are accepting a life that is going nowhere and the future is grim.

Recruitment/search firm owners who lead successful and joyful lives have achieved this by choosing beliefs that support and empower them on their journey to a successful business.

An example of how beliefs from the past shape our lives today:

On May 6, 1954, Roger Bannister became the first person to run a sub-4 minute mile. Prior to this monumental event, the 4-minute mile barrier had developed such a mystique around it that some even considered it a physical impossibility and it hadn't been broken – ever!

In fact, the scientists of the day claimed that if a man ran a mile in under four minutes he would die from a heart attack as his body would not be able to take it.

But the next month (after Bannister had broken this myth), the barrier was again shattered by John Landy, and in the following few years broken by almost a dozen more runners. Now there are almost 900 men who have run a sub-4 minute mile.

Over the past century, advancements in training techniques, equipment and track surfaces have continuously whittled away race times. But, what led this one man to break the record when he did, when many others had tried and failed? The answer is simple: his belief that he could.

Our beliefs determine how high we set our sights

Roger Bannister believed he could run a sub-4 minute mile, and so aimed for this goal with all the direction and focus he could muster.

Go here www.recruitmentsalesrecipe.co.uk/inner-circle and complete the questionnaire to identify your limiting and empowering beliefs.

Don't let the past equal the future

I recently watched the Disney movie 'The Lion King' and there is a scene that reminded me of the many recruiters I talk to on a daily basis.

Rafiki, the wise monkey, went to find Simba, the main character. Simba was the rightful heir to the pride, but had been encouraged to run away and never return after a freak accident that killed his father. His dishonest uncle told Simba that the death of his father was Simba's fault.

When Rafiki found Simba, he begged him to return to the pride and restore law and order in the animal kingdom.

"I can't return to the pride," said Simba.

"Why not?" inquired Rafiki.

"Because of what happened in the past. I am ashamed of what I have done and I cannot go back."

At this point Rafiki swung his walking stick with a vengeance and smacked Simba right between the eyes.

"Ouch, what is that for?" shouted Simba.

"It does not matter, it is in the past," said the wise monkey.

"That maybe so, but it is hurting now."

"Ah, but you see, this is where opportunity lies. For you can focus on the pain, and question the reason of the past, or you can go beyond the pain and learn from the past." At this point Rafiki went to hit Simba again with his stick, and this time Simba ducked.

The moment Simba ducked, he had realised that it was better to learn from the past than to hold onto it.

Many recruitment/search firm owners are bit like Simba, they let the past dictate their future. *Don't fall into that trap!*

Recruitment and Search firm owners will say things like: *"I tried that once, and it didn't work."*

I hear this a fair amount as they are looking for some magic bullet to grow their business.

"How often did you try?" I ask. *"Once, twice?"*

What would you say to a child who said, *"I tried that once and it didn't work"?*

Just because you asked a hiring manager for a retainer and they refused, doesn't mean that they will never pay a retainer. All it illustrates is that this particular hiring manager will not pay a retainer to you, at this stage.

The same applies to techniques and strategies you can use to generate more leads and increase your earnings. As I mentioned earlier, to get success requires work, practice and persistence. It takes time for you to master the skills and time for you to have the business you desire.

So **learn from past actions that did not work**, rather than holding onto to them to justify your behaviour today, otherwise it simply adds weight to your *"butt"*.

There is a gift waiting for you from the kind and extremely generous 'Renegade Recruiter'

Before you go any further, make sure you go to
www.recruitmentsalesrecipe.co.uk/inner-circle
and get the tools, templates and scripts which will enable
you to influence your prospects and candidates effortlessly
and with integrity, so that you can increase
your personal earnings.

This normally sells for £297.00/$465.00 but you can get it
FREE! Simply go to;
www.recruitmentsalesrecipe.co.uk/inner-circle

Part 4: Your Big Butt

If I had a pound for every time I heard, *"Yeah, but..."*

That is often what I hear when I share with recruitment/search firm owners the 'new methods' for generating leads.

- ⮑ *"My market is different, and this type of marketing will not work."*

- ⮑ *"I am not comfortable putting my head above the other recruiter, I may get shot down."*

- ⮑ *"I don't know how to do it."*

As you can guess, I could go on, but the fact is; the only but is your *"butt"* getting in the way. And that *"butt"* is simply **fear.**

Fear of it not being perfect, or something going wrong, or fear of failure. Remember I spoke about your beliefs in the previous section? Well, fear of failure could well be a 'limiting belief' that you've learned from your parents or carers.

Look, whatever you think about what you have discovered so far, all of this it is not based on my opinion or some theory, this is what the top firms are doing. But don't take my word for it, test it, then you have opinion based on fact rather than your fears.

What is fear?

Fear is a chain reaction in the brain that starts with a stressful stimulus and ends with the release of chemicals that cause a racing heart, fast breathing and energised muscles, among other things. This is also known as the fight-or-flight response.

The stimulus could be a snake, a gun at your head, an auditorium full of people waiting for you to speak, the sudden thud of your front door against the doorframe, or even the FEAR of rejection, the FEAR that someone may criticise you, or question what you are doing or saying.

The brain is a profoundly complex organ. More than 100 billion nerve cells form an intricate network of communications that are the starting point of everything we sense, think and do. Some of these communications lead to conscious thought and action, while others produce autonomic responses.

The fear response is almost an entirely automatic reaction; we don't consciously trigger it or even know what's going on until it has run its course.

It's dark outside, and you're home alone. The house is quiet other than the sound of the programme you're watching on TV. You see it and hear it at the same time. The front door is suddenly thrown open. Your breathing speeds up. Your heart races, your muscles tighten.

A split second later, you know it's the wind. No one is trying to get into your home.

For a split second though, you were so afraid that you reacted as if your life were in danger, your body initiating the fight-or-flight response that is critical to any animal's survival. But really, there was no danger at all.

How the fear of failure is holding YOU back

Fear of failure was first uncovered in the 1960s by psychologists, one of whom was John Atkinson. Working at Stanford University, USA, Atkinson conducted a series of experiments on children. By setting them reward-based tasks in order to test their motivation, he noticed that they divided into two camps: those focused on winning the reward, who approached the task with what he called a *'need for achievement,'* and those focused on their seemingly inevitable failure, who had what Atkinson termed as a *'fear of failure'*. This was based on their desire to avoid the public humiliation of failure.

In one experiment, the children played a game of hoop-the-peg, with greater rewards offered for greater distances. The 'need for achievement' kids stood a challenging but realistic distance from the peg - adding concentration if they failed. Those with 'fear of failure', meanwhile, stood either right on top of the peg or so far back that failure was almost certain.

Of course, those choosing the impossible distance effectively disguised their fear of failure, not least because everyone failed at such a distance. Yet that was the better response. Many of the fear of failure kids became disruptive, indicating that they didn't care for the game, with some even trying to halt the entire process.

But FEAR doesn't stop there. Every day I talk to owners and directors of recruitment and search firms, and every day I hear and see examples of fear of failure:

"Yeah but I am a perfectionist so I will not send out any marketing until it is perfect."

Just think about that statement for a moment, any sane person will tell you that 'perfection' doesn't actually exist, so the moment you go for 'perfection' you know you are sabotaging your success.

"I cannot market to my potential prospects, it will annoy them."

You can market to them and annoy the odd one, or you don't market to any of them and get no additional business. Which would you rather?

As I have said numerous times…

"Success is a choice, your choice."

The fact is, if the methods you are using right now are getting you the results that you want, then keep doing them. If you are not getting the results you want, then would it be worth doing something different?

I am often asked this question: *"How often should I sell and market to my potential prospects?"*

The answer is quite simple really; you sell and market to your prospects until they buy, die or tell you to go away. If you have not got one of those three responses, you are not selling often enough to them.

I once read that FEAR really stands for:

False

Evidence

Appearing

Real

For many recruiters, it's the fear of *rejection* that inhibits their ability to ask for the business, the fee they really desire, the exclusive, or the retainer.

It is FEAR that makes some recruiters accept low fees, it is FEAR that stops the recruiter from walking away from a business deal when they know in their heart of hearts that they shouldn't be doing business with that prospect.

It is FEAR that makes the recruiter ask, *"how high?"* when the client says, *"jump"*.

What is fascinating about the whole aspect of fear is that most fears are learnt.

We are born with a fear of loud noises and a fear of falling. But basically, all the other fears you and I have, have been learnt. And in most cases, FEARS are quite irrational.

Take the fear of rejection...

When a prospect says *"no"*, for instance, to you (asking for a retainer), it simply means that they don't see the value in paying you a retainer. It is nothing personal; they haven't rejected YOU, just what you have proposed. There is a massive difference.

I once had a mentor called Peter Thomson and he had a mantra when it came to selling and marketing.

He called it the 'Chelsea Mindset' or 'SW3' (which is a district of London, UK).

- Some Will

- Some Won't

- So What?

Besides which, if every prospect said *"yes"* to everything you asked for, you wouldn't be able to handle all the business anyway, so some rejection is good for you.

If you had no fear of rejection you would simply ask for the business, the retainer, the exclusive, or the higher fees.

All research suggests that the amount of business you have is simply a reflection of how much you fear rejection. So the less you fear rejection, the more you will earn. By the same token, the more you fear rejection, the less you will earn.

It is worth reading the last two lines again.

The fact is, MOST of your marketing will be ignored and fail. Some of the marketing campaigns our prospects have embarked on have resulted in a 2% response. Now that means that 98% of people had no interest in their recruitment offering. Most of your attempts to get your prospect to buy from you will result in rejection and failure, but that's OK!

World Famous FAILURES that you may have heard of:

Michael Jordan

Michael Jordan is considered one of the greatest basketball players of all time. In his brief bio on NBA.com, he is described as 'single-handedly redefining the NBA superstar', and yet to get there he openly admits to failing more than most. In a famous ad campaign launched by 'Nike', Michael is quoted as saying he has:

➲ Lost almost 300 games (that's more games than many NBA players have court time in).

➲ Missed over 9000 shots at goal (again, more shots than an average NBA player even takes).

➲ 26 times he was given the ball to take the game winning shot and MISSED.

Jordan goes on to say that the reason he has succeeded boils down to his constant failure, and that he has used failure as motivation to shoot for success. In other words, Jordan viewed failures as stepping-stones towards success; his shooting average was just below 50%, so to score he would have to take two shots, one to fail and the other to score.

Thomas Edison

Thomas Edison is considered the greatest inventor of his time. He was responsible for over 1,000 different patents. Some were refinements of previous inventions, but many were completely new ideas. Edison is famous not only for his inventions, but also his attitude to failure.

In his mind, failure was simply another stepping-stone on the road to success. Unlike Michael Jordan, however, Edison's rate of success was significantly below Jordan's 50% average.

But unlike the average person, Edison continued to try and try again. As the famous story goes, Edison failed to refine the light bulb (one of the few creations he merely refined but did not invent) so many times it took him 2,000 attempts to perfect. However, rather than accepting failure 1,999, times he is quoted as answering questions on his failures as rather: *"I have not failed, I have just found 9,999 ways that do not work."*

Winston Churchill

During the First World War, Churchill was the chief proponent of the invasion of Turkey, which is now known as the Gallipoli campaign.

The idea was to create a southern link to England and France's eastern ally, Russia and provide the struggling country with materiel assistance. This, of course, was a total failure.

During the Second World War, Churchill was also responsible

for the decision to occupy Norway. The invasion of Norway (or perhaps 'military occupation' is a better term) was challenged and defeated by Nazi Germany. Perhaps the main reason for this failure was the defeat of British naval surface power by German air power. Just like Gallipoli, it could be said of Norway, *"a nice idea, but it didn't work"*.

Despite all this, Churchill was one of the greatest leaders of the 20th century and certainly one of history's great orators.

"The only thing we have to fear is fear itself." ~ Franklin D. Roosevelt

So go chill and ask for what you truly desire...

There is a gift waiting for you from the kind and extremely generous 'Renegade Recruiter'

Before you go any further, make sure you go to
www.recruitmentsalesrecipe.co.uk/inner-circle
and get the tools, templates and scripts which will enable
you to influence your prospects and candidates effortlessly
and with integrity, so that you can increase
your personal earnings.

This normally sells for £297.00/$465.00 but you can get it
FREE! Simply go to;
www.recruitmentsalesrecipe.co.uk/inner-circle

Part 5: The Narrower The Niche, The Broader The Appeal

Answer this very important question: *"Who is your ideal client?"*

If your answer is, *"everyone"*, then keep reading, as this is <u>critical to your long-term success</u> as an owner of a recruitment/search firm.

Recruitment companies that try to be all things to all people will have significantly higher marketing and client acquisition costs, never really establish a strong prospect base from which to grow, and often disappear before achieving profitable growth.

Recruitment/search businesses with too large a target market (i.e., every business in the world) struggle to get any clients at all, and here's why: not understanding who your prospects *really are* keeps you from being able to better serve them.

Most recruitment and search firms take the shotgun approach to prospecting, by simply going after any and all prospects and all job orders. In other words, they try to be *all things to all people* and never establish a niche or core competency.

The old days of calling on 2000 potential prospects with a hope that something comes up are long dead. It's all about calling on prospects that meet your predefined qualification.

How often does your firm say *"no"* to a new job order?

Not only must the prospects have a logical reason for engaging your firm, you must have a logical reason for taking on the business.

For example, marketing to a one-man business, run from home, is a waste of your valuable time and money (I'm sure that example is obvious to you). The point I'm making is really to encourage you to define what is your market and why?

What is your market and why?

Here's how you can answer that question and get more prospects:

Authority

A critical factor is: does the person have the authority to engage you? So often recruiters will spend time with the line manager, getting all the details of the role, only to find out that all buying decision are made via HR.

If the hiring manager doesn't make the decision on which recruitment/search firm to use, you have wasted a lot of time and money. You must get the authority first, and then discuss the details of the role, not the other way round.

Paint a picture

If you've never completed an exercise on identifying your prospects, I encourage you to do one now. Grab a notebook or start typing.

Answer the questions fully, and get creative if you're not sure of the answers. The goal is to paint a picture of who your ideal prospect is.

Go to www.recruitmentsalesrecipe.co.uk/inner-circle, get the 'ideal client' document and do the exercise.

You're likely to have other types of prospects, but focus on the ones that you enjoy serving and want more of.

Consider what makes this prospect perfect in your mind. You can physically draw a person or cut images and words from a magazine to visually define them.

Shedding the rest

The purpose of this exercise is to ensure that all your marketing, web copy and messaging targets *this specific type* of prospect and candidate.

Again, if your marketing is too generic, and you're trying to be all things to all people, you'll fail. Zero in on writing your marketing directly to this ideal prospect, and you'll find that you instantly attract more like them.

The secondary purpose of this exercise is to get rid of the client types that you don't want. You know the ones – you lose money working with them simply because they take up a lot of your time. Or they buy on price and price alone.

By properly identifying who your ideal prospect is, you will set your company on the right track to getting more (and better) business.

The secret to attracting, as opposed to hunting, your ideal client is to understand what makes them tick and what triggers them to go looking for someone like you.

Niching your marketing message

One of the common problems with recruitment and search firms is the mixed message that is communicated to potential prospects and candidates.

Once you have a clear picture of what your ideal client looks like, your communication becomes so much more effective. You stop trying to be all things to all people and become the *'go to recruiter'* in your niche.

One thing that strikes me about the recruitment/search firm owners who are struggling to attract all the business they want, is that they don't actually know who their ideal prospect is. Sure, they may have some inkling as to what market they operate in, but I'm talking about a careful analysis here.

The top recruitment/search firm owners have a very strict set of criteria that a potential client must meet before they'll even get into a conversation with them. And it pays because it means they don't have to spend any time with the tyre kickers.

Some recruitment/search firms are happy to work with any old business as long as they have the ability to pay, and some people won't even set ability to pay as a requirement. *(I'm talking about you, if you're constantly working on non-exclusive/non retained job orders and wonder why you can work your ass off and STILL end up not getting paid.)* The consequence of this is that they're left with the scraps of business that the top firms didn't want. The startling fact is, the average contingency recruiter will fill 25% of the job orders they work on. That means that for 75% of the time they are working, they will never ever get paid for the work they do!

Crazy, right?

I am sure you would agree that this is not a particularly good business model.

This is partly because the recruiters think you can't control who you attract into your business, and they're desperate for any and every prospect they can get. But if you think that, you're dead wrong.

The top performers don't just go after anybody, they're very selective about who they do business with. This is because they know that **doing business with the wrong people can end up costing them more money than it makes.**

If you build a business that is willing to go after just anybody, it's almost impossible to avoid doing so based on price, which is a losing battle because there will always be someone willing to do it for cheaper than you are.

Think about it; if you know *exactly who your best set of prospects are*, you can then use specific demographics to select the people who match up well with that profile, and then invest all of your marketing efforts to attract only those best prospects.

And when I say best prospects, I mean the people who buy based on the best value rather than the best price.

When you have a prospect list full of only the best, you can't help but have a more profitable business. You work less but earn more, and the people you're working with become long-term friends as well as business contacts.

A true win / win.

There is a gift waiting for you from the kind and extremely generous 'Renegade Recruiter'

Before you go any further, make sure you go to
www.recruitmentsalesrecipe.co.uk/inner-circle
and get the tools, templates and scripts which will enable
you to influence your prospects and candidates effortlessly
and with integrity, so that you can increase
your personal earnings.

This normally sells for £287.00/$465.00 but you can get it
FREE! Simply go to;
www.recruitmentsalesrecipe.co.uk/inner-circle

Part 6: *"Will You Please Stop Calling Me!"*

If you have known me for any length of time and have read any of my eBooks, blogs or other publications, such as, *'The 7 Deadly Threats to your Staffing and Recruitment Business'*, you will know only too well my opinion of making those dreaded 'cold calls'.

By the way, this is not just my opinion, it is also based on the findings of some of the top recruitment and search firms in the world.

For many 'old time recruiters', cold calling is the only way to get business, so let me clear up this myth once and for all - *That is complete and utter B.S!*

Other ways of attracting business may be:

➤ Referrals

➤ Most placeable candidate/marketing out candidate (MPC)

➤ Networking

➤ Reference check

➤ Word of mouth

➤ Hope marketing - this is where you just HOPE business will come your way. (Not recommended for long-term success.)

The fact is, there are over 100 different ways that you as a recruiter can generate business, without making a single cold call. It's not possible to cover them all here, but look out for my other books on this subject, which are coming soon.

The latest research carried out in 2013 found that the average hiring manager in IT gets between 5-10 'cold calls' a day, that is as many as 200 cold calls a month, or 2,400 cold calls a year. Can you imagine that?

I have a close friend who is vice president of HR in the automotive industry, and she says: *"If I were to take every call from every recruiter, all claiming to be different yet all saying the same thing, I would spend 60% of my day on the phone talking to these guys."*

I have no reason to think that it is any different in any other niche. And ask yourself this, has a hiring manager every said to you: *"I really enjoy having my day interrupted by you trying to sell me recruitment"*?

An interesting study on 'cold calling'

What you're about to read is quite revealing.

A recent study by the Kenan-Flagler Business School at the University of North Carolina concluded that some 80% of B2B decision makers in the United States absolutely, positively <u>will not buy</u> from companies that cold call them.

Another study by the Keller Research Center at Baylor University in Texas reveals some interesting numbers too.

The study was based on a group of 50 experienced and qualified salespeople, who made a total of 6,264 phone-based cold calls over a two-week period.

- 72% of the calls were outright rejections.

- 28% of the calls were productive. That is, people who didn't hang up right away, showed some interest (some even gave referrals), or asked to be contacted later.

But what's most interesting is that the majority of the two-week study period was spent working on and following up with this 28%.

The time that went into it was extraordinary and very eye-opening. Out of that 28%, 1,774 calls resulted in 19 appointments and 4 sales.

4 sales out of a total of 6,264 cold calls made!

As some of you know, there are more easier and satisfying ways for getting business.

So what can you do to get more business and increase your personal earnings without 'cold calling'?

All will be revealed, but first, let's look at why potential prospects will never ever buy from your firm, and what to do about it.

"Your prospects will buy from you when they are ready to buy, not when you are ready to sell to them."

This is really important - and most of your competitors out there have no idea about this - so when you get this, you will have a head start on them.

Firstly, there are **four main reasons** why a potential client will never ever engage you:

1. They don't KNOW you

2. They don't TRUST you

3. They don't LIKE you

4. They don't have any NEED for what you are offering

Let's say you are a search firm and your average fee is 20k of your local currency.

Why on earth would a hiring manager spend that kind of money with someone they don't know, like or trust, especially if they have no need for what you are offering? Makes sense, right?

Every time a hiring manager makes the decision to engage a recruiter, it is so they are better off after making the decision. From the hiring manager's point of view, they can engage your firm, or one of the many other recruitment/search firms out there offering a similar service. The hiring manager will decide to use the company that they believe will <u>benefit them best</u>. The fact is as stark and as simple as that.

Most recruiters don't get this and go storming in trying to sell their service with no regard for the client and absolutely no understanding of the prospect's needs/wants, and if the prospect even wants to buy.

Imagine this scene, you are at home with your family and the phone rings. It's Joe, the local plumber and the call goes something like this: *"Hi, my name is Joe and I am your local plumber. I am calling all the homes in the area to see if you have any leaks we can repair?"*

Would you respond with, *"Thanks for interrupting my time with my loved ones"*? Or would you say, *"Listen, buddy, when I have a need for a plumber I will give you a call"*?

Well, that is what thousands of recruiters are doing every day.

Here are some disturbing headlines from UK newspapers regarding cold calling:

"Bosses of nuisance call companies could be hit with £500,000 fines in a government crackdown on unwanted calls and texts."

"Up to one billion British families receive cold calls each year, leaving many elderly people 'too scared' to answer the phone, ministers said."

"Culture Minister Ed Vaizey said nuisance calls were a 'plague' on families and had to stop."

"The government's Nuisance Calls Task Force said new rules should be introduced to make company bosses responsible for cold callers causing 'severe distress' to families and business owners."

Added to that, many recruiters don't actually enjoy making these calls.

So the point is: you don't enjoy making them, your prospects don't like receiving them and the UK government is trying to put a stop to them. Added to which, research suggest that most prospects are unlikely to give a cold caller business. When you 'cold call' you are seen a PEST, when your objective is to be the WELCOMED GUEST.

Can you spot the difference between the two?

Stop being the PEST and become the WELCOMED GUEST

To understand how to do this, you need to know about a fundamental marketing problem at the heart of nearly all recruitment/search firms in the world.

The problem is this: *how does a company balance its marketing and sales efforts?*

You see, in most recruitment/search firms, the marketing department's role is to get the leads, and the sales department's role is to call on the leads and close the sale. (That is if the recruitment/search firm has a marketing department, and the majority don't.)

The top performing recruitment/search firms are using more than *100 different methods to get leads,* so that they are on the 'welcomed guest' list.

Think about this, if they are using 50 methods for getting leads and they get 10 leads per month from each method, that is 500 hot leads a month, every month.

This is while the mediocre and struggling recruitment/search firms are using a couple of methods for getting leads. Who do you think gets the most business?

But also, in between getting the lead and closing the sale, there's a huge gap. When you close the gap, you'll make the shift from hunting mode to harvesting mode, and your profits will skyrocket.

To make the shift, you need to recognise right now that:

A. The business development job doesn't end when the lead is acquired.

B. The sales job doesn't begin and end with a 'check it out' phone call to each prospect.

C. Someone has to be in charge of warming the leads that aren't hot right now, but will be hot down the road.

In other words, if you want to make more placements, the functions of marketing and sales must come together. Otherwise, your marketing effort amounts to simply flushing money down the toilet on leads that aren't hot right now. Imagine tearing up hundreds in your local currency and throwing the cash away.

And if you're a solo recruiter, then you're the marketing department *and the sales department*, no wonder it's so tough to take your recruitment/search business to the next level.

To sum up this problem of the gap between marketing and sales, think of it this way; every business has a lead-generation department (marketing) and a lead-closing department (sales), but they're lacking a lead-warming department.

Permission marketing

So, now that you understand the task in hand, let me give you 9 critical steps to make the shift:

1. Send relevant, valuable information to every prospect regularly, relentlessly and frequently. You need to be doing this until they buy, die, or tell you to go away (in other words relentless marketing).

2. Communicate with prospects/candidates efficiently, aside from the normal, time-consuming, one-on-one telephone methods.

3. Log all communications between your office and the prospect/candidate in an organised fashion, so that anybody that follows up can see what has happened.

4. Create reports/eBooks, etc., of high value content which you can send to prospects/candidates on request. Example:

'7 Questions To Ask A Search Firm Before You Engage Them.'

5. Track the progress of each lead through the sales pipeline, so you always know where every lead stands. ☐

6. Follow up with every prospect that requests your free report. Ask for a 10-minute telephone meeting with the prospect.

7. After the telephone meeting, implement an automated email campaign in order to be at the forefront of the prospect's mind.

8. Get the business.

9. Repeat all of the above.

The good news is that it's actually very easy to do all of this, *and* you can have it done for you *effortlessly with an automated emailing system.*

Whether you're a solo recruiter or a multi-site search firm, it is imperative that you make this shift. And when you make this shift, **you'll be amazed at the results. 80% of prospects who request your free report will agree to a 10- minute telephone meeting with you.**

You do the math…

If you generate 2 leads a day, or 40 leads a month, and of those 40 new leads, 80% agree to a 10-minute telephone meeting with you, what could that mean in terms of profits for your business? Think about that. Theoretically, you could speak to 32 decision makers about their future recruitment needs and wants in a month.

And let's say you only convert 3% of those into business. That is approximately one new client a month, every month.

Now answer these questions...

➲ *When you get a new client, on average how much will they spend with you in the first 12 months?*

➲ *What will that client spend with you over the lifetime of the relationship?*

➲ *Can you see how you can double your sales in the next 12 months?*

So if your average fee is 10k of your local currency, that equates to an additional 120k in the first year, and if you fill five roles for each client in the lifetime of the relationship, **that is an additional 600k.**

And now that you know the number, you now know how to scale it up.

So, based on the numbers above, if you wanted t*hree new prospects a month*, you know *exactly* what you would need to do to get them. The famine and feast that most of your competitors endure is completely eliminated forever. Your personal earnings are now predictable and scalable; you now have a secure future.

The bottom line is this: you'll close more deals, make more money, and do it all in less time.

There is a gift waiting for you from the kind and extremely generous 'Renegade Recruiter'

Before you go any further, make sure you go to
www.recruitmentsalesrecipe.co.uk/inner-circle
and get the tools, templates and scripts which will enable
you to influence your prospects and candidates effortlessly
and with integrity, so that you can increase
your personal earnings.

This normally sells for £287.00/$465.00 but you can get it
FREE! Simply go to;
www.recruitmentsalesrecipe.co.uk/inner-circle

Part 7: Size Does Matter!

In February 2004, Mark Zuckerberg was thinking about size.

He had just created his first crude version of what was then called thefacebook.com, a universal website that could be used by students to contact people around Harvard University.

The first thing he did when he finished the website was to tell a few of his friends about it. Two of them recommended that he should acquire a mailing list, and promote the concept to those on the list. Mark took their advice, the website generated over 1,000 registered users within 24 hours, and within a month more than half of Harvard undergraduates had registered.

It kick-started a business that today is worth over $200bn!

Getting more people on your 'list'

Connect with them on LinkedIn - for the sake of repeating myself, the four main reasons why prospects will never buy from you are.

- They don't KNOW you
- They don't LIKE you
- They don't TRUST you

- They have no NEED for what you do

For those that don't know about LinkedIn;

LinkedIn is a social network site designed for the business community. At the time of writing this book, there are 340 million users on LinkedIn, with a new member coming on every 2 seconds. LinkedIn currently operates in 200 countries, so a lot of your potential prospects use it. Not all of them, but a significant number.

With a basic LinkedIn membership, when you connect with someone (ideally the decision maker), they become your first connection and you get access to their contact details which can include: email address, telephone number and postal address.

Another very important reason to connect with prospects on LinkedIn is Facebook. And not many of your competitors are even aware of this relatively new method for getting more business.

Yes, that's right, **Facebook!**

You see, when you are connected with someone on LinkedIn, 99% of the time when you click on their contact details, you will see their email address.

This, my friend, is priceless! Because you can then load those email addresses into Facebook and if the potential client uses the same address for their Facebook account, then you can display your eBook to them using Facebook Pay Per Click (PPC). In other words, you display your ad for your eBook and if your potential client has no interest then there is no cost. If the potential client is interested, then you pay Facebook a few dollars. Yes, only a few dollars per lead, and you are generating leads all the time. And of course, you're not making any 'Cold Calls'.

And before you say… *"My Prospects are too sophisticated to be on Facebook".*

Consider this…

There are now over 1.28 billion people and 30 million brands using Facebook each quarter. Your prospect is more likely to be on Facebook than LinkedIn.

With increased competition facing recruitment/search businesses, especially smaller ones, not using Facebook to generate leads is like not using a telephone. It can be done, but it makes things so much more difficult than it needs to be.

Facebook facts and statistics:

✓ 30 million businesses now have a Facebook fan page.

✓ 19 million businesses have optimised their fan page for mobile.

✓ Businesses are paying 122% more per ad unit on Facebook than they did just one year ago.

✓ 399 million Facebook users only use it on their mobile phone each month.

✓ 829 million people use Facebook on a daily basis, an increase from 802 million last quarter.

✓ 654 million people use Facebook on their mobile phone on a daily basis, an increase from 609 million last quarter.

✓ 1.32 billion people log in to Facebook at least once each month, an increase from 1.28 billion last quarter.

✓ 63% of Facebook users engage with it on a daily basis.

✓ 1.07 billion people use Facebook on their mobile device each month, an increase from 1.01 billion last quarter.

✓ The average Facebook user spends 40 minutes a day on the platform.

✓ 12 billion messages are sent per day through Facebook.

✓ Facebook Messenger is used by 250 million people each month.

✓ Businesses spent $2.66 billion on Facebook advertising, an increase from $2.27 billion last quarter.

✓ Mobile advertising revenue represented 62% of advertising revenue during the second quarter of 2014, a 41% increase year over year.

✓ Facebook users bought $234 million dollars' worth of virtual goods and gifts via Facebook over the last quarter.

✓ Facebook engagement topped 1 billion during the World Cup.

✓ Twice as many people now watch videos on Facebook in their feed compared to just six months ago.

✓ The majority ($1.175Billion) of Facebook's revenue comes from US and Canada, with Europe coming a close second at $757 million.

✓ People search 1 billion times per day on Facebook.

✓ 80% of the top apps on iOS and Android use Facebook Log in.

Nurturing your list

Often when I talk to owners of recruitment/search firms, and ask them what the size of their database of potential prospects is, those that are struggling will say something like, *"I have quite a large list of 200-700 potential prospects."*

Believe me, that is not a large list, that is positively small.

Why?

Well, there is a concept called the 'now buyers', which is estimated to be between 5%-10% of your list. The 'now buyer' is a buyer that is ready to buy in the next 30-90 days.

So, if you have a list of 700 and 3%-10% of them are 'now buyers', that means you have 21-70 potential buyers, at best, to go for. Now bear in mind that every single one of those buyers is likely to have a relationship with one of your competitors.

So the size of your list *does matter.*

It is recommended that you have a list of at least *2000 potential prospects* per fee earner in your business. (If you think there are not that many potential buyers in your niche, then you need to find another niche with the potential for you to make some good money.)

In fact, there is a good chance that you already possess some massively valuable lists – perhaps without understanding their true value. The lists I'm talking about are your lists of clients, including *old* clients

For many recruitment/search firms, a huge opportunity is being missed. All this frantic marketing generates prospects, but not all prospects are ready to buy now. In fact, the majority aren't ready to buy immediately. However, with effective communication this *'list of clients'* will come to you when they are ready to buy and I talk about this in much more detail in Part 9, *'Converting Those Leads'*.

One of my 'Elite Clients', Colin Edge from EMC Projects, shared a story with me, which in my experience is typical for many of the successful recruiters we work with.

Colin has accumulated a list of prospects of approximately 4000. Like many recruitment firms, he rarely, if ever, speaks to them, and rarely, if ever, emails them. Like many recruitment/search firms we work with, he was reluctant to email his list of 4000 in case - and I quote, *"we piss them off"*.

The bare fact is this: if you never ever communicate to your list of potential Prospects and you wait for them to call you, then you will have a long wait.

When you communicate with your list and offer them something that solves their problem, then some of them will request the information and then you have got yourself a lead.

In all the years we have been sharing this with our clients, every single client who has emailed their prospects more frequently has seen an increase in sales. So test it for yourself and see the results.

Anyway, back to Colin

So Colin committed to test the theory of communicating more frequently with his list of potential prospects. He implemented what he called the *'Motivating the List Technique'*, and he emailed them six times in 10 days offering high value content in the form of a report called *'The Perils of Taking on Contractors in Today's Competitive Market'*.

From an initial list of 4000, he did *'piss off'* some prospects. He also cleansed his list, as many of the names on there were out of date, and he increased the number of contractors out by 16% in just over two months.

Have you ever achieved a 16% increase in contractors in two months without making a single 'cold call'?

To quote Colin, *"I am quite happy with the prospects that no longer wish to receive my emails, because I need some companies that I can headhunt into, besides which, if 'pissing off' some prospects increases the number of contractors by 16%, then I must do it more frequently."*

Colin did what the majority of his competitors will never do. He tested it and then had the facts regarding what worked and what didn't.

Colin now knows exactly what to do to increase his profits by 16% in the next 90 days.

"If you can't measure it, you can't manage it." ~ *Peter Drucker*

Most of Colin's competitors will listen to their friends, colleagues, associates and social media trolls who say that you mustn't communicate with your prospect too frequently. As a consequence, they won't get any additional sales.

And with that, many recruitment/search businesses have forgotten just how valuable these lists can be. Often, these lists get treated as the mere by-product of 'real' marketing – they become wasted leads, failed prospects and the unconverted. Yet the truth is, your early surge of conversion just pays for the cost of the marketing – the real profits come from the second, third and subsequent wave of conversions.

These subsequent waves only come if you value, nurture and develop a powerful marketing STRATEGY for your list.

Let's consider some hard facts:

- ✓ Many prospects today are slow buyers, slower than ever before, and they are often not buying until you have 'touched' them 7 to 10 times (sometimes up to 50 times!).

- ✓ This process can take 3 to 24 months.

- ✓ Most sales people give up after 3 or 4 rejections – way before most buyers are ready to transact. Therefore, you create expensive leads that are wasted.

- ✓ It is widely reckoned that attracting new prospects will cost you 5 to 6 times more than keeping an existing client.

- ✓ According to Bain and Co., a 5% increase in client retention increases profits by 25% to 95%.

- ✓ Gartner Group says that 80% of your company's future revenue will come from just 20% of your existing clients.

- ✓ The most responsive lists you can use for your marketing are, in this order: your prospect list and your lapsed list. These are "free" (you already own them).

Email Marketing

With email broadcasting, the cost of staying in touch with your list has plummeted from up to £1.00 per contact, to just a few pence.

Email broadcasting (to your lists) is the top marketer's secret weapon. If you can work and monetize a list properly, you can dominate the market and crush your competitors.

The chances are that if you don't build, value, nurture and market to your lists with a properly developed strategy based around email broadcasting, you'll struggle to compete and win.

You may develop the belief that Google Ad Words is too expensive, that Direct Mail is too costly, and that marketing is hard. In the meantime, your savvy competitors will be quietly building and growing their lists, working their communication strategies and plans, and making huge sales volumes to existing clients, previously unconverted leads, and even to their lapsed prospects.

Savvy recruitment/search firm owners know how to 'monetize' lists:

✓ They understand that it can take 5, 10, 20 even 50 (high quality) touches before prospects are ready to buy.

✓ They understand that they have to intelligently stay in touch with high quality information – to add value, to educate, to inspire and to sell.

✓ They understand the *MFR rule* – the people most likely to spend more with you tomorrow are those who have spent the MOST, most recently and most frequently.

✓ They have integrated the *'forgotten'* art of growing, nurturing and gaining market *'pre-eminence'*.

Without a warm database of prospects and candidates, you don't have a prospect base, you have a prospect graveyard, and you will be broke.

Getting the message *right*

➲ Your personality is important.

➲ Your prospects need information.

➲ They need repetition.

➲ They need education.

➲ They need variety and frequency.

➲ They need to hear the right message at the right time.

But if you want phenomenal results, you need to give them what they want. And that does not include your monthly newsletter all about you and your business, or the fact you have taken on a new consultant, or that your receptionist is pregnant or you're moving office. *Your prospect couldn't care less.*

They want your personality. They want you to be real with them. They want you to be straight up, helpful, sincere. They want your spin, your angle, your advice and your perspective. They don't want corporate B.S. They want YOU!

And when you give them what they want and combine it with what they need, you've got something spectacular, even entertaining. You've got permission to converse freely with your prospects, to help them with the things they need, to offer them the services you provide that make their life easier, better, more successful.

Story of the 'speed-reading expert' who was broke

I remember a few years back meeting a guy who goes by the name of Dan Bradbury. You may or may not have heard of him, but he's best known here in the UK for training coaches, to be coaches.

He's one of the first people I learnt from when starting out.

But way before he was doing that, you might have known him better for his speed-reading skills. After coming 2nd in the 'Speed-Reading World Championships', he was soon considered to be one of the world's fastest readers and started a business teaching other people how to do the same.

He had developed a technique that allowed him to teach almost anyone to increase the rate at which they were able to read and take in information.

His business didn't quite go to plan, but his speed-reading strategy worked! And it's something I still use today.

The basis of it is this:

You flick through the book from start to finish, almost fanning the pages as you go. Then you go to the front of the book to the contents page and read the title of each chapter, just so you begin to get an idea of what each section is about…

Then you start the book as you would normally, using your finger as a guide as you move across each word.

Try it, it really works.

Anyway, back to Dan Bradbury.

Like so many other businesses, he struggled to really get it off the ground. People just weren't buying, or at least not enough of them to create the lifestyle he wanted for him and his family.

It wasn't that what he was selling didn't work. I still use his speed-reading technique, as do many others.

It wasn't that people didn't want or need what he was selling, either. If you think of the student market alone, there are more than enough people who would want to speed up the rate at which they read.

It wasn't his pricing structure, either. I could spend days talking about price and why it doesn't necessarily stop people buying but we'll come back to that another time.

The reason he struggled was because of his marketing.

You could be the world's best recruiter or search firm owner:

- You could have the best service…

- The best team

- The best candidates

- The best CRM…

- The best price…

- The best systems…

None of that's going to put food on the table and money in the bank. Sure, all those other things are important, especially if you want your business to ever reach its full potential, but they count for nothing unless you can actually get leads in your pipeline and prospects to pay you money, both of which are a direct result of good marketing!

The better you are at it, the more leads you generate and the more prospects you get. Sounds fairly straightforward, but it can be frustrating to see so many recruitment/search firm owners push marketing to the bottom of the pile, treating it as an optional task that they can do 'when they get time'.

No!

You need to make time. If you don't, one of two things will happen!

You'll either stay as you are, perhaps doing 'OK' but deep down knowing you're not really pushing yourself or your business to its full potential.

Or...

You'll end up eventually going out of business completely, with nothing to show for all the hard work you've been putting in.

The choice is yours.

Get this right and you will have more business than you can imagine.

There are three and *only* three factors that really have an iron grip on the profits of your recruitment/search marketing effort.

This simple, but incredibly powerful formula is: *The right message, to the right market, at the right time!*

Most recruitment/search firms miss one, two or all three of these factors, and as a result have very ineffective marketing. Heck, just miss one of them and you're looking at the wrong end of a marketing disaster.

Also, some recruitment/search firms magnify these problems by spending money on advertising, with no direct response offers at all.

Some web designers and marketers say things like, *"It's about the brand."* This is known as mass marketing or **'brand advertising'**.

The goal of this type of advertising is to remind prospects about your brand, as well as the products and services you offer. The idea is that the more times you run ads for your brand, the more likely people are to have this brand at the forefront of their minds when they go to make a purchasing decision.

If you've seen the ads from major brands such as Coca Cola, Nike and Apple, you'll have experienced this type of marketing. The vast majority of advertising falls into this category. There's no doubt that this type of marketing is effective, however, successfully executing it takes a lot of time and a ton of money, and the majority of search/recruitment firms just don't have this.

It requires you to saturate various types of advertising media, e.g., TV, print, radio and internet on a very regular basis and over an extended period of time.

Want to know what message to send out? Don't panic, I'm coming to that next, in part 8!

Have a well-defined 'Call To Action' (CTA)

So often recruiters will write to their prospects. It will be a well-written letter or email, well designed and laid out. However, they get little and, in some cases, no response whatsoever. All because they didn't follow what is the most critical rule when communicating.

Tell them what you want them to do!

So if you are marketing a candidate and you want them to call you to arrange an interview, 'tell them'.

Your nurturing emails that your potential client will receive should tell them to email you or call you. You can ask them to book a 10-minute telephone meeting with you. Whatever it is, tell the reader what you want them to do, otherwise they don't know!

If you can't measure it, you can't manage it

In ALL your marketing activity, you must be able to track and measure its success, otherwise you will never know what works and what doesn't.

Consider this: you have a meeting with your bank manager because you require funds for further expansion. You tell the manager that you want to spend 20k of your local currency on some 'branding'. No doubt your bank manager will ask, *"What will be your return on investment for this?"*

Well, that question is impossible to answer with any accuracy, because you won't be able to manage who sees what, when, and if that was the reason they got in touch. Yet there are many 'gurus' out there who will tell you it is all about the 'brand'.

Quite simply, save your money, your time and your sanity.

Direct response marketing for recruitment and search firms

The Top 6 reasons to use direct response marketing

1. It's trackable. That is, when someone responds, you know which ad and which media was responsible for generating that response. This is in direct contrast to mass media or 'brand' marketing – no one will ever know what ad compelled you to buy that can of Coke.

2. It's measurable. Since you know which ads are being responded to and how many sales you've received from each one, you can measure exactly how effective each ad is. You can then drop or change the ads that are not giving you a return on investment.

3. It uses compelling headlines and sales copy. Direct response marketing has a compelling message of strong interest to your chosen prospects. It uses attention-grabbing headlines with strong sales copy that is '*salesmanship in print*'.

4. It targets a specific audience or niche. Prospects within specific verticals, geographic zones or niche markets are targeted. The ad aims to appeal to a narrow target market and speaks directly to them.

5. It makes a specific offer. The offer focuses on the prospect rather than on the advertiser, and talks about the prospect's interests, desires, fears and frustrations. By contrast, 'brand marketing' has a broad, one size fits all marketing message and is focused on the advertiser.

6. It demands a response. Direct response advertising has a 'call to action', compelling your client or candidate to do something specific. Of these responses, it also includes a 'capture' facility. This means that when the prospect responds, their contact information is captured so that they can be contacted beyond the initial response.

The objective of your marketing efforts is to *generate leads* – people you can follow up with. When you convey the right message, to the right market, at the right time, this will happen.

When they are hot they are HOT

Every time you run a marketing campaign, the leads you generate can be divided into three groups:

1. Leads who are ready NOW (Hot): Likely to use a search/recruiter in the next 90 days.

2. Leads who are not ready now but will be ready soon (Warm – these leads are CRITICAL to your success): Likely to use a search/recruiter in next 90 plus days.

3. Leads that may never be ready (Cold or Bad Leads).

The problem is you can't divide the leads into categories because you don't know which leads are HOT or otherwise. So, you call every lead once or twice and then you spend the time with the leads that look like they're going to close.

Every smart recruiter that works on commission does this – they go for the low hanging fruit!

If you DO reach the lead and the timing isn't quite right, i.e., in the next 90 days or so, put a system in place to constantly follow up. Remember, just because they are not ready to buy NOW, doesn't mean they are not EVER ready to buy.

Timing

Most recruiters will tinker with their message and their market and end up with something that works okay. But they forget how critical timing is in the whole mix.

Remember the quote I stated earlier:

> **'Your prospects will buy from you when they are ready to buy, not when you are ready to sell to them.'**

And this means, by definition, you have to be in front of potential prospects and candidates when they're ready to buy. In other words, you have to follow up with them consistently! Because if you don't, some other recruiter will get the business.

And if you want retained search it is imperative that you get to the prospect before the world and his wife does. And guess what? That someone else who lands the business will be your competitor, who either followed up consistently, or got lucky enough to cross paths with your potential client/candidate at the right time. (I am sure you have experienced that.)

The one thing you control in this situation is staying in front of the prospect.

For most recruitment/search business owners this can be a challenging task. I talk with recruitment/search business owners all the time who tell me they know they should stay in touch, follow up and 'be there' for their prospects and candidates, but they just can't seem to get a system in place or the time to do that.

The fact is, 'follow-up' is gut wrenching, time-consuming, tedious and can be a labour-intensive task that is almost impossible for the human mind to keep straight. So, most recruitment/search businesses have concocted half-baked schemes, spreadsheets, tickler files, software programs, and who knows what else, to help them with this all-important business function.

Remember, most recruitment/search firms are mediocre!

So they do follow-up like this (if they do it at all) and most of their schemes and techniques are spectacularly unsuccessful. As a result, recruitment/search businesses all over the world leave *huge piles of leads and money on the table* every month. They continue to throw away good money, only to let the majority of prospects drop through the holes at the bottom of the bucket because the timing wasn't right for them.

So, it kind of tells you something must be done. According to recent findings, over 95% of Recruitment/Search firms do not consistently follow-up with their prospects and candidates.

But the good news is that you can easily annihilate this problem, and when you do, you'll make more placements and increase your personal earnings.

Now you understand the importance of follow up.

Let's look at...

Your USP

Master this one question: *"Why should I work with your firm?"*

This is the single most important question because the right answer to it, as I'll demonstrate, is the key to the marketing vault. It doesn't just marginally increase things, it multiplies them far beyond the ability of most people to even conceive. It is that important

Now the technical term for the answer to this question is USP. It stands for Unique Selling Proposition, which differentiates you from all competition, direct and indirect. And here's the question.

"Why should your prospect choose to do business with you versus any and every other option available?"

And when you have a great answer to that question, you can turn things upside-down.

Words that built a multi-million business empire

I'm going to give you a model to use, a model of one of the best Unique Selling Propositions invented in the last two decades.

So, what you want to do with this model is lay it down next to your Unique Selling Proposition, and see how they compare. And if they don't compare very well, then this one's a good place to start to build a better one.

A college kid invented this particular Unique Selling Proposition model. Here's the story:

There were two kids who were orphans. They had no family resources, no athletic ability, no scholarships, but were both determined to go to college. They found a crummy, miserable, stinking little retail business on the edge of campus, and it was on the brink of failure. Its owner was only too happy to lease it to them with no money put down, just to get it out from under his feet and to relinquish the ongoing bills.

The two kids then ran this business. One of them went to school during the day while the other one worked the business, and then they switched. The other one went to school at night, and vice versa. They planned to do everything in the business themselves.

Shortly into the plan, the business continued to hemorrhage money. One partner bailed out and the other one dropped out of school, determined to honour his commitments and make this work. This is when he came up with a Unique Selling Proposition.

And on the strength of his USP, he almost immediately turned a failing business into a successful one. Pretty soon, he had multiple outlets. He dominated his city, he dominated his state, and he eventually dominated North America. And in less than five years, according to Fortune magazine, he became one of the 1,000 wealthiest citizens on the planet, all thanks to his eight-word USP.

These 10 words were so powerful that for a decade you could go out anywhere in North America, stop 100 people at random on the street, and ask, *"What's the first thing that comes into your mind when we say... blank..."*

That's called marketplace dominance. That's what this kid got. He turned his entire industry upside-down, and had everybody chasing him, trying to catch up. You can do it too, with the lever of a great USP.

His was: *'Fresh, hot pizza delivered in 30 minutes or less, guaranteed.'* And on the strength of that, Tom Monaghan took a crummy little corner pizza joint and built Domino's Pizza.

When you analyse it, there are a number of things to spot. Firstly, how narrowly he defined his position in the marketplace. Tom didn't try to be all things to all people. Secondly, there's no mention of Mama's recipe from the old country. There's no mention of only using sun-dried tomatoes gathered on the east side of the mountain on a Tuesday.

There's not even any mention of good pizza! There's truth in advertising after all.

There are many ways that I teach my clients how to build a strong USP.

The one Tom used is called *'Opportunity Gap Exploitation'*. He identified the one thing in his industry that everybody did badly, that annoyed the consumers the most, and he focused on it, fixed it, and made it the core of his marketing message. (Pizza delivery times, if you've missed it!)

Secondly, he used meaningful specifics, rather than vague generalities. Tom Monaghan didn't say, *"I'll get your pizza to you soon... fast... quick... quicker than the other guy... faster than a speeding bullet..."* Tom said, *"Set your watch. It will be there in precisely 30 minutes or less, or your money back."*

We call that gutsy, accountable marketing. Very few marketers and business owners are ever willing to do it, for obvious reasons. Those who do gain incredible leverage in the marketplace. And there's case history after case history to support it.

Thirdly, he gave a guarantee. Tom took all three of those things and knitted them together in this tight, concise little statement, which gave him the leverage to turn one little business into a global empire. You may not want a global empire, but you might like the leverage.

Think about why people should do business with you versus any and every other option available to them in your niche? How's your answer? How's your marketing message?

Uncovering your USP

Here's how to uncover your USP and use it to power up your sales:

- Put yourself in your prospect's shoes.

- Know what motivates your prospect's behaviour and buying decisions.

- Uncover the real reasons why prospects buy from you instead of a competitor.

Don't get discouraged. Successful recruitment/search business ownership is not about having a unique recruitment/search service, it's about making your product stand out - even in a market filled with similar services.

To help you create a powerful and compelling recruitment/search USP go to: www.recruitmentsalesrecipe.co.uk/inner-circle and get the USP workbook...then create a USP that blows your competitors away.

There is a gift waiting for you from the kind and extremely generous 'Renegade Recruiter'

Before you go any further, make sure you go to
www.recruitmentsalesrecipe.co.uk/inner-circle
and get the tools, templates and scripts which will enable
you to influence your prospects and candidates effortlessly
and with integrity, so that you can increase
your personal earnings.

This normally sells for £287.00/$465.00 but you can get it
FREE! Simply go to;
www.recruitmentsalesrecipe.co.uk/inner-circle

Part 8: Let's Get Emotional Baby

Do you want to know the secret to getting prospects to want to buy from you more than you want to sell to them? You tap into their **EMOTIONS.**

The top guys understand that ALL buying decisions are based on emotion and justified with logic. This is really important, so let me repeat that.

All buying decisions are based on emotions and justified with logic

Most people believe that the choices they make have resulted from a rational analysis of available alternatives. In reality, however, emotions greatly influence and, in many cases, even determine our decisions.

In his book, *'Descartes Error'*, Antonio Damasio, professor of neuroscience at the University of Southern California, argues that emotion is a necessary ingredient to almost all decisions.

"When we are confronted with a decision, emotions from previous, related experiences affix values to the options we are considering. These emotions create preferences that lead to our decision."

In other words, your past emotional experiences will affect your decision making in the future.

Damasio's view is based on his studies of people with brain damage. The connections between the 'thinking' and 'emotional' areas of their brains had been damaged. They were capable of rationally processing information about alternative choices, but they were unable to make decisions because they lacked any sense of how they felt about the options.

Not convinced...?

Do you really think that when a family spends £20k on a new kitchen it is because the old one wasn't working and they needed a new one? The decision to spend £20k on a new kitchen is because they WANT to not because they NEED to. The decision is based on the emotions of ego, status, recognition, even wanting to 'out do' the neighbours and/or family.

What is the time?

Have you ever noticed that the watches and clocks found in product photographs and advertisements usually show the time 10:10? If you haven't, pay attention the next time you see an advert.

If you have noticed this, do you know why 10:10 is the default time for watch photographers? There are a number of visual advantages to having the hands set at the 10:10 positions. One is that the hands are kept from overlapping. Having them on both sides of the watch face ensures that the hands themselves are visible and can be appreciated. The 10:10 hands look "happy" due to the fact that they resemble a smile. Timex used to use the time 8:20 in its product photos, but eventually decided to turn that "frown" upside-down.

No emotion, no sale

You, as a seller of recruitment/search, must tap into the emotions, needs and wants of the buyer/hiring manager. We fundamentally make all of our decisions based on emotion, not logic. Logic supports our emotions and is used to justify our decisions after we have made them. Logic plays a part, but emotion is the core ingredient. Show me a recruitment sales person with no emotion during the presentation and I will show you an underperforming consultant.

Once you identify the target audience for your marketing messages, you need to consider which emotional triggers you can connect to those messages.

Here are some common emotional triggers that you can tie into your sales messages when presenting.

Fear: Fear is an emotion that can be used in a wide variety of sales messages. As a recruiter, you could ask the question, *"What are the implications for you as a hiring manager if you are unable to find the right candidate for your company?"*

Guilt: Consumers are easily affected by messages that trigger emotions of guilt. Nonprofit organisations use the guilt trigger effectively in copy such as, *"Don't let them suffer anymore."* Do you remember Live Aid?

Trust: Trust is one of the hottest trends in sales. If your prospect doesn't trust you, you will not get the sale.

Belonging: Few people truly want to be alone. Human nature dictates that most people want to feel like they belong to a group, and prospect can be influenced to engage a recruiter if that recruiter is positioned as an authority in a particular niche and works with similar companies. This translates as, *"you're part of the family"*.

Competition: The old adage of 'keeping up with the Joneses' is an adage for a reason. Many prospects are affected by a competitive desire to feel equal to or better than their peers. When marketing a candidate, tell the prospect that he or she is also talking to their main competitors.

Spend some time crafting your presentation so that you are tapping into your prospect's emotions.

No emotion, no sales

There is a gift waiting for you from the kind and extremely generous 'Renegade Recruiter'

Before you go any further, make sure you go to
www.recruitmentsalesrecipe.co.uk/inner-circle
and get the tools, templates and scripts which will enable you to influence your prospects and candidates effortlessly and with integrity, so that you can increase your personal earnings.

This normally sells for £287.00/$465.00 but you can get it **FREE!** Simply go to;
www.recruitmentsalesrecipe.co.uk/inner-circle

Part 9: Converting Those Leads

So the prospects know you, and have raised their hand and indicated that they have some interest in your recruitment/search offering.

You have implemented a systemised marketing process in your business and your recruitment/search firm gets warm leads via permission marketing. In other words, you offer prospects a report/eBook or something else of high perceived value that will help them solve their problem, such as: *'The 7 Questions You Must Ask A Recruiter Before You Spend Any Money With Them'*, which I've mentioned before.

The prospect requests your eBook, so clearly they are at least thinking about doing some recruitment.

What you are about to discover will mean you will have conversion rates of up to 60%. Yep, from first meeting to obtaining the business, you will achieve that up to 60% of the time.

Just for a moment, imagine what that would mean to you if 60% of your meetings led to some business.

However, not everyone who requests your eBook will have an *immediate* need for your service, or will be the decision maker when it comes to engaging your service. If you're pitching to people who truly don't need or can't buy what you have to sell, you're wasting your time and money. So taking the time to qualify your sales enquires *before your go and visit them or launch into a sales pitch* is important.

So, you send them your eBook (using an automated process) and then phone them and leave a message with their PA or a voicemail telling them that you have sent the eBook they requested.

You then email them regularly *(ideally 4 emails per week)* to nurture the relationship and position yourself as an authority in the sector. You also send them a letter via post. The regular contact you make with them will get them to **know you**, **like you** and **trust you**.

Now, interestingly, when following up leads, there are some fundamental mistakes that recruitment and search firms make which unwittingly stop them from getting the business. I've outlined the 7-step conversion model that will help with that.

The 7 step conversion model

1. Have a specific 'Desired Outcome' - *Unless you know where you're going, how will you know when you have got there?*

So, from the very outset, you must know what you want to achieve from the follow up. Sure, you want to get the business, but what needs to happen before that to ensure you get it?

Also, who will be responsible for following up on ALL leads that come in?

It is recommended that someone is assigned that responsibility. That way you have some accountability.

An ideal 'desired outcome' should be a 15-minute telephone meeting with the person who requested the eBook to establish their responsibility and what their search/recruitment requirements and timetable might be.

There are a number of benefits to a telephone meeting:

- ✓ Less resistance from potential prospects
- ✓ Cost effective
- ✓ No need to travel
- ✓ Saves time
- ✓ Save money
- ✓ Takes the relationship to the next level
- ✓ Improves conversion rate

2. Develop a 'Professional Greeting' - Don't just say, *"hello…"* and jump into your telephone presentation without taking a breath or allowing the other party to participate.

Your greeting should be professional. Begin with Mr, Mrs or Ms as in *"Good morning, Mr Smith"* or *"Good afternoon, Mrs Jones"*. Everyone else says *"Hello"*. Be different, be professional.

3. Introduce yourself and your company - *"Prospect, my name is XX from (name of firm). We help companies like yours to find top candidates (make it specific for the industry that you recruit in)."*

4. Ask Permission - Always ask if this is a good time for them to take the call. *"Do you mind if I take 30 seconds of your time to explain why I am calling, then you can decide if we take this call any further?"*

5. Remind them that they requested your eBook and that is why you are following up - It's best if you can provide the purpose within a question. *"You recently requested my eBook"* (Name of eBook).

6. Do not ask them if they have read the eBook. Instead ask, *"I don't suppose you have chance to read it yet, have you?"*

(I know that sounds rather negative, but the fact is, 80% of the prospects that request your eBook will never ever read it. They will scan it on their screen with the intention if reading it later.) But by positioning your introduction this way, should the client say, *"Yes, I have read it,"* you can reply with, *"great".*

But if they haven't say, *"I can appreciate that, you must be busy."*

(See part B, on step 7 below, to continue the script.)

7. Script that will get you a telephone appointment.

"Hi Mr, Mrs or Ms Prospect, my name is XX from (name of firm). We help companies like yours to find top candidates (make it specific for the industry that you recruit in). Do you mind if I take 30 seconds of your time to explain why I am calling, then you can decide if we take this call any further?"

Shut up and wait for a response.

The responses you are likely to get are:

"Sure, that's fine."

"That was kind of you to ask."

"What is this call about?"

Explain that you are happy to tell them what the call is about if they have 30 seconds now, or at a time that is good for them.

If they agree, then continue with:

"You recently requested my eBook (name of eBook), now that you have received it I don't suppose you have had a chance to read it yet, have you?"

Shut up and wait for a response. Then you can continue with:

Part B) *"The reason for the call is that many of your competitors in your industry have also requested the report/eBook (name of book). If you are anything like them, then you're well aware that it is very much a candidate's market, with the top candidates spoilt for choice. This makes it extremely difficult for you to recruit the best candidates.*

The implications are that you end up with second best and that does not reflect well on you. Not to mention the problems it creates for the business. So I guess if I could show you a way to overcome that, you would be open to it, wouldn't you?

So to help you, we are giving five companies only a free 10-minute telephone consultation on how to attract the top candidates in the industry

This is what you will get in our discussion: '5 ways to attract top candidates without using a recruiter.' 'What top candidates are really looking for, and it is not what you think.' 'How to write ads that attract top candidates', an 'Overview of salary expectations for the top candidates' and 'What you must never ever say to a candidate during the interview.'"

Then give them an alternative day for the meeting.

"Which day would suit you best for this telephone meeting to give you and your company a competitive edge, Monday or Tuesday?"

If you get an objection like:

"Send me your terms."

Use the objection formula

Agree: *"I appreciate you would want me to do that."*

Answer: *"I will get them to you after this call, before I go."*

Ask: *"If I could help you overcome the number one challenge when trying to identify and attract top candidates (or job title), what would that be?"*

Shut up and wait for a response.

If the response is something you can help them with...

Example: *"Finding the right candidates with appropriate background and experience."*

Your response is:

"So I guess if I could help you overcome that problem, you would be open to that, wouldn't you?"

Shut up and wait for a response

Then give them alternative dates.

"Which day would suit you best for this telephone meeting to give you and your company a competitive edge, Monday or Tuesday?'

Shut up and wait for a response.

"Great, shall we say 10am on Monday then? I will drop you a line to confirm."

Why scripts are important

Often when I am coaching Recruitment/Search firm owners, we share with them powerful sales scripts that work.

Sometimes there is some resistance to using scripts, as they will claim one of the following

"My team will sound like robots."

"You can't build genuine rapport by reading a sales script."

"You can't hire top recruitment consultants who have been successful and tell them to us a scripts."

"Scripts sound insincere."

But scripts are so important, and here's why...

A few years ago I was at my friend's office he owned a local newspaper and he had invited me his office to conduct an interview with local business leaders. As I sat with him in the office his phone rang, it was a 'cold call' from a recruiter I overheard her pitch, it went like this...

"Hi my name is Lindsay from your local recruitment agency, I don't suppose you have any job orders you would like us to fill"

My friend replied;

"You are right I don't." and simply put the phone down!

That my friend is a *lousy script,* which will more often than not get that sort of response.

The most successful recruitment/search firms insist that all their consultants use a script that works.

Why you should be using a sales script

Refine your methodology

Designing sales scripts for you and your team encourages you to really think things through. By developing a sales script, writing things out word for word, you bring structure and clarity into your selling process and your teams thinking.

Raise your entire teams performance

You can create a constant feedback loop if you involve your whole team.

Get your top consultants to share success stories, best practices and new creative ideas. There's a lot of great sales knowledge in the room that typically is just stuck in someone's head.

Improvements spread faster throughout your whole team.

When you have a sales script everyone is using, and one Recruiter deviates and tries a different approach, and find it consistently performs better - that improvement now gets shared!

The whole team learns this way, rather than it being just one creative sales genius. You continuously elevate the skill level of your whole team.

By having a script, you basically create a safety net for shitty days that prevents people from performing shitty.

Developing a scalable sales process means you are no longer relying on recruiting the top billers.

You'll train, manage and scale your sales team better. Building an effective sales operation is not about finding individual sales superstars. It's about creating an all-star team. You don't want to be the team that has the best individual players; you want to be the strongest team.

A sales script helps you to bring new people up to speed faster, train and benchmark them better and just generally scale your sales faster. With a good system/sales script in place it means you don't have to constantly be on the lookout for the top billers in the industry. Now you recruit individuals on their intellect, and personality and know that when they follow a sales script that works they will enjoy the same success.

The point is, a powerful and profitable 'Sales Script' will help you and your team close more sales, make more placements and increase your personal earnings as the owner of the business.

There is a gift waiting for you from the kind and extremely generous 'Renegade Recruiter'

Before you go any further, make sure you go to
www.recruitmentsalesrecipe.co.uk/inner-circle
and get the tools, templates and scripts which will enable
you to influence your prospects and candidates effortlessly
and with integrity, so that you can increase
your personal earnings.

This normally sells for £287.00/$465.00 but you can get it
FREE! Simply go to;
www.recruitmentsalesrecipe.co.uk/inner-circle

Part 10: The 'Sales Structure'

Your potential prospect needs to be sold to in an orderly, organised, momentum-building manner. There is a 'sales structure' that is very reliable, and when used effectively, it makes the client want to buy more than you want to sell.

Planning your sales call

To ensure that you obtain the outcome you wish to achieve, YOU must plan your sales call. Some salespeople are blessed with a natural ability to just do it and sometimes get away with it. Having worked with some of the top recruiters in the world, the one thing they all have in common is that they plan.

The fact is, even the most gifted politicians, when answering tough questions live on TV, have a plan, and this is the case even if they have been at the game for decades. Planning your sales calls (and other client interactions) is still necessary, and it still improves your results.

Without knowing the desired outcomes of the meeting, you are less likely to obtain them.

To ensure you achieve all of the desired outcomes of a sales call, you should plan it. Make a list of the outcomes that you need to achieve.

That same list of outcomes will provide you with an opportunity to ask yourself some questions that will make your sales call more effective, as well as making it more valuable for your ideal candidate/ client.

Planning the outcome helps you to decide what you need to do to obtain it.

By identifying the outcomes, you can also identify what you are going to have to do in order to obtain them.

Some possible desired outcomes might be:

- How to access other decision makers/line managers?

- The decision making process for engaging a recruiter?

- An understanding of what is important for the client when engaging a search firm.

- What are their frustrations about using a search firm?

- What does the client believe are the key skill sets required over the next 9 months for the company to achieve its goals?

- Understanding of when the prospect is likely to recruit next.

- What does the client like about their current search firm?

- What does the current search firm do that they would like to see less of?

- Date of next meeting.

Questions for YOU:

- How much time do you presently spend planning your sales calls?

- Even if you are gifted at thinking on your feet, why is it still important to plan to achieve the outcomes of your sales calls?

- Have you ever left a sales call and forgotten something that you wanted to accomplish?

- How much time should you spend preparing for a sales call?

- What do you need to see, hear and feel to know it is a good call?

As impressive as your ability to think on your feet may be to you, your dream client expects you to have a plan.

It is more impressive to your potential client that you have developed a thoughtful, logical and professional plan for the time that they have invested in you. A short written plan takes about 10-minutes to develop. If you have a must-win, mission critical sales call or interaction, spending half an hour planning your call will be an awesome investment of your time, and you will produce greater results for having done so.

One final and important thought - *Your potential client doesn't want or expect you to wing it.*

Shut up and listen

Have you ever heard the expression, *"You have two ears and one mouth so you should listen twice as much as you speak"*? What about, *"Silence is golden"?*

It doesn't matter if you haven't, you will still be able to take advantage of this under-utilised ability. Chances are that you have participated in meetings or conversations where people have talked and talked and talked for no apparent reason other than to show-off in front of colleagues or their boss. When you sit back and listen, you often notice that despite the noise, the conversation isn't moving forward. In these instances, people are concerned with demonstrating their knowledge, their communication ability, their decision-making power, etc., rather than really communicating.

Many recruiters find silence during a sales conversation a difficult concept to manage. People do find silence extremely uncomfortable, especially when a period of it engulfs a conversation, be it an interview or a sales presentation. However, silence is a very powerful weapon when you want to influence someone.

To make it absolutely clear; *it is not easy and it takes discipline and effort, yet, when used properly, it can help you gain more sales.*

Here's how you can use silence to negotiate a better deal for your business.

When you pause for three to five seconds before responding to a comment or statement they have made, the other person will often volunteer additional information that they have otherwise kept to themselves.

Here's an example…

Several years ago, I received a phone call from someone who wanted me to speak at an upcoming executive search event in the USA. We discussed the dates, the location, the other speakers and what they wanted me to cover. During the telephone conversation, I sensed that the caller wanted to tell me something.

So I asked this question: *"I am curious, what else do you want to share with me about the event?"* I then remained completely silent. A moment later, the caller replied, *"We only have a budget of $2000...is that okay?"*

At that time, I often spoke at events for expenses only with the understanding that I could sell my books at the end. However, the person I was talking to was used to paying for speakers. The five seconds of silence helped to generate a small sale of $2,000, all because I kept quiet and listened.

A client of mine is the owner of a recruitment firm that recruits software sales people. He told me of a situation when he was discussing the terms of a recruitment campaign with a new prospect. His prospect asked if he could get a better fee, as they wanted to recruit at least three sales people. My client remained silent as he considered his options. After several seconds of complete silence, his prospect said, *"Well, if you can't do that, it's okay."*

Since that day, my client always pauses after a demand for a concession has been made. He figures this one action has earned him thousands of additional dollars in fees.

When I worked as a search consultant and I used to interview candidates, a tactic taught to me was called the *'tell me more pause'*. After a candidate responded to a question, I smiled and looked at them expectantly. In most cases, the candidate volunteered more information.

Another powerful method is to simply say, *"tell me more,"* and shut up!

We are afraid of silence

Let's face it, silence feels awkward. A sales encounter can be, at times, a slightly tense experience. When we're nervous and encounter silence we feel an almost irresistible urge to fill it.

When a client raises a question or objection, or doesn't respond right away, we may feel it's our job to say something more. However, to make the sale, saying nothing can be far more effective than anything we might have said.

Silence is powerful

I heard an interview on the radio several years ago in which a police detective was talking about interrogation techniques. The detective mentioned that after a suspect answers a question, their interrogators often simply maintain silence. The detective said that the suspect would often provide vital information. In the pause, the nervous suspect keeps talking to avoid the quiet.

Obviously, the sales process has a different end in mind than an interrogation, but the power of silence is just as important in selling.

There's an old adage in sales that goes, "He who speaks first loses." I don't like the idea that the hiring manager is losing if you let them speak first (in the art of sales and influencing, it must be win/win), but there are moments in sales where letting your client speak first will result in a positive outcome for you.

When to use silence

When you ask for the business, simply ask the question: *"What do we need to do to get started?"* Then shut up and listen.

Another powerful question is, *"What do you need to ask me before we get started?"*

1. When a client raises an objection or question

Don't feel that you have to instantly jump in and answer questions or offer immediate solutions to objections. Frequently you will get valuable information from your potential buyer by saying nothing at all. If you remain silent and expectant, as if you are waiting to hear more, the buyer will sometimes answer the question, or further elaborate on the concern. There's no law that says you have to jump right in with a response. Try and keep the ball in the buyer's court.

2. When negotiating with a prospect

Silence can be particularly useful in negotiating fees. Allow a pause after a client makes a suggestion to see if they will soften their request for a concession. Allow for silence after you make a counter-offer.

3. After asking for the business

Silence is particularly effective after asking for the business. If you keep talking, you're preventing your buyer from having the opportunity to say "yes". After you have asked for the business, you should never be the next one to speak. Wait for your client to respond, even if the pause is long and uncomfortable for you.

Use silence – close more sales

As with all sales tools, silence should be used, tested and measured. The most successful recruiters use the power of silence to great effect.

What you must measure after every call

☐ Did you research the prospect prior to the call?

☐ Did you learn something about the person and their business before the meeting?

☐ Did you send an outline of the agenda to the prospect before the meeting?

☐ Have three value-added points been prepared?

Answer the three important pre-call questions:

A. What is the goal of the call?

B. What do I need to find out during the call?

C. What's the next step after the call?

Qualifying

☐ Find out who the decision makers are by asking, *"Who else, besides yourself, might be involved in the decision-making process?"*

☐ Ask what process they normally go through when considering a new recruitment/search firm?

☐ Find out what their time frame is.

☐ Find out their specific needs.

☐ Ask: *"If you could change something about your current recruitment/search firm, what would it be?"*

Surveying

Ask *open-ended* questions (who, what, where, when, why, how, how much, tell me about it, describe for me).

Ask about the corporate structure.

Ask about the prospect's role within the company.

Other examples:

What's important to them in terms of recruitment/search firms?

What's interesting to them? (Then focus on that.)

What risks do they perceive?

How can we help to solve their problems?

What do they think about our company?

What do they like and dislike about their current provider?

How are industry trends are affecting them?

Ask *what if* questions.

What would they like to see from a recruitment/search firm?

What are their short-term and long-term goals?

How can I become their most valued recruitment/search provider?

What is our next step?

Establish a specific follow-up schedule.

Handling Objections

Did you:

- ☐ Listen to the entire objection?

- ☐ Pause for three seconds before responding?

- ☐ Remain calm and not defensive?

- ☐ Meet the objection with a question in order to find out more?

- ☐ Restate the objection to make sure we agreed (communication)?

- ☐ Answer the objection?

Did you complete the six-step process?

1. Listen

2. Define

3. Rephrase

4. Isolate

5. Present solution

6. Close (or next step)

Closing

Did you?

- ☐ Get the prospect to identify all possible problems that might be solved by your service?

- ☐ Get the prospect to identify the value of solving the

identified problems?

☐ Get an agreement that the proposed solution provides the values identified?

☐ Ask for the business (*"Why don't we go ahead with this?"*)?

The 8 step recruitment sales process

This is a process that has been developed over many, many years of selling, as well as watching and listening to top performing recruiters from around the world.

I have taught these methods and ideas to recruiters across thousands of markets.

Here are the eight stages:

1. Beginning:

This is where we focus the hiring manager's mind on the conversation that is about to take place.

2. Feedback on what you know:

You should already know a lot about the company from your research and you should have an overview of the industry. Remember, you have to instill confidence.

3. What is the situation?:

Understand their role, responsibilities and their challenges when recruiting.

4. Implications:

What are the implications of these challenges for the hiring manager and the company? Ideally, you should have at least two 'implications', one for the business and one for the 'hiring manager'.

Example questions: *"What are the implications for the business if this problem continues?"*

To establish personal implications, ask, *"What are the implications for you on a personal level if this problem continues?"*

5. Needs and Wants:

This is essential before presentation. So many recruiters launch into their 'pitch' about their services before they have obtained enough information from the hiring manager in order to understand the prospect's wants, needs and motivation. In the gathering stage you will begin to understand the pain the prospect is experiencing.

To confirm their 'needs and wants', ask, *"So, if I could show you a way to overcome your hiring problems and the implications you mentioned, I guess you would be open to that, wouldn't you?"*

> *"Seek first to understand, then to be understood."* ~ *Stephen Covey*

6: Presenting:

This is where we focus on the reasons why the prospect will make a buying decision.

7. Concluding:

This is actually taking the order, getting the sale.

8. Relentless follow-up:

This is where we check that the delivery of the service has lived up to the promises we've made, or in the case where we didn't win the business, it's to keep in touch so that we do win the business when the client is ready to buy.

There is a gift waiting for you from the kind and extremely generous 'Renegade Recruiter'

Before you go any further, make sure you go to
www.recruitmentsalesrecipe.co.uk/inner-circle
and get the tools, templates and scripts which will enable you to influence your prospects and candidates effortlessly and with integrity, so that you can increase your personal earnings.

This normally sells for £287.00/$465.00 but you can get it **FREE!** Simply go to;
www.recruitmentsalesrecipe.co.uk/inner-circle

Part 11: Sales Meetings

A sales meeting can be face-to-face or over the telephone. Either way, there is a process and technique that, when followed, will ensure you are more successful.

Meeting preparation

Provide background to what you do (keep this brief) and provide your USP (discussed earlier, in part 7).

Get an understanding of their business, where they are now and where they would like to be.

This must include:

✓ Type of business

✓ Their USP

✓ Number of employees

✓ Turnover

✓ Profit

✓ What they would like to be doing in terms of sales.

✓ What they believe is stopping them from achieving that.

✓ What other skills/resources are required by the business over the next 6 months to ensure that the company objectives are achieved.

Researching your prospect

Imagine you are not feeling too well so you decide to go to the doctor. As soon as you walk into her surgery she asks you to strip down to your underwear and get on the treatment table. As you are doing this, she launches into the fact she has been a doctor for 10 years and most of her patients are still alive!

I suspect you would be a little nervous in this situation, and may even consider suing her for malpractice, as she has asked you to strip down without asking any questions to establish what your problem is.

Diagnosis without analysis would be considered malpractice in the medical profession, and the doctor would be fired.

That is precisely what most recruitment/search firms do. They don't ask the client to strip down to their underwear, but they do launch into what a great firm they are and why the client should engage them.

It amazes me how few recruiters actually take the time to learn about their prospect before they launch into their presentation.

Where to get the information.

LinkedIn

LinkedIn is a gold mine for prospect research. If you can only research your prospect on one platform before your call, make it LinkedIn. Find prospects on the network, and check out each of the following areas of their profile:

⮑ Experience at their current job – Most people list primary job duties or major projects they've worked on. This can help you get a sense of what falls into their remit, and what doesn't.

⮑ Experience at their former jobs – Customise your messaging based on their career history. Is this there first time making this kind of purchasing decision, or have they done it many times?

⮑ Shared connections – If you have a connection in common with your prospect, make sure to bring it up during your conversation and ask how they know this person. This could be a referral opportunity.

⮑ Groups – Click through to their groups to see what's being talked about.

⮑ Recent activity – Take a look at what your prospect has recently shared, and where.

Prospect's Twitter Account

If your prospect has a Twitter account, you should spend a few minutes on their page to get a sense of what they're interested in. Look through their recent Tweets, read a handful of the articles they've recently retweeted and look into an issue they've posted about.

Company Twitter Account

What kind of content and messaging has the company been promoting? Understanding how the company is presenting itself to its prospects can help you better understand how to present yourself to your prospect.

Company Press and Media Release Page

Scroll through recent press releases and see if anything major has been announced, such as leadership changes, product releases, financial statements, events or prospect wins.

Competitor Press and Media Release Pages

If a competitor has made a significant announcement within the past few months, that will colour the way your prospect looks at your offering - either as a competitive advantage, or an unnecessary expense in the face of more pressing priorities.

Financial Statements

If your prospect works for a public company, it might be a good idea to check out its most recent financial reports. This will give you an idea of how the company is performing.

Blogs

Read what your prospect reads, and read what your prospect writes. If your prospect maintains a blog, be sure to read at least the last few posts and comment on them during your call. In addition, visit the websites of popular industry blogs and peruse the latest posts to learn more about the trends and challenges shaping the environment.

Facebook

Facebook is more of a personal social network, still, it might be helpful to check out your prospect's profile to pick up a few titbits about them. Make sure you weave these into the conversation naturally, or you risk giving off an overly personal vibe. Also, this is another good place to see if you have any friends in common.

Google the company

Conduct a search on the company to bring up any news stories that they've kept off their press page - good or bad. Be sure to select third-party publications that are high quality and reliable.

Google the prospect

Search your prospect's name in quotes to surface any other information about them that might've fallen through the cracks. What is their situation? Understand their role, responsibilities and challenges when recruiting.

Ask about their role and responsibility

This will help you discover if the person is the decision maker, and who else may be involved.

How do they feel about their current service?

Once you have the basic information about their current product, dig for what their likes and dislikes are about it. This information is incredibly useful when you reach the presentation phase, since you'll already know what their preferences are.

What are the timescales?

Even if a prospect is interested in your service, they may not be able to buy right now. Other times, it'll be something like a contract that hasn't expired yet or a key person who's out of the office.

It is not what you say, it's what you ask that gets results

There is this perception that good selling recruitment it is all about the 'gift of the gab'. There is nothing further from the truth; the best sales people ask good questions so that the prospect tells the recruiter what they are looking for, rather than the recruiter telling the prospect what they do.

Successful recruiters ask better questions and, as a result, get better answers. Most recruiters ask lousy questions that cripple their results.

Here are some questions that will help you get the business:

- How soon would you want to put this in place?

- If I show you how you can save money/ time/improve yourself, etc., would you be ready to start today?

- In an ideal world, when would you like the candidate to start?

- What do you think is the typical notice period for this type of candidate?

- Ideally, when would you like to be making an offer to the candidate?

- How does your company purchase a service of this type?

- How does your company make the decision to engage a recruiter?

- What are the organisational relationships that influence the decision?

- Who are the people typically involved in this decision-making process?

- What are the concerns or roadblocks that could crop up down the road and get in the way of us working together?

- What timely and relevant issues are going on internally?

- What do like most of all about your current recruiter?

- What would you like to see your current recruiter do less of?

- What are the implications if that was to continue?

- Who else in your company should I be presenting to and following up with?

- What will it cost you and your company if you keep things the way they are today?

- I am curious, Mr/Ms Prospect, do you want the top candidate that is not actively looking, or do you want any candidate that is desperate for a job?

Here are some questions you should be asking, and what you must know BEFORE you present your offering.

Find out what their number one and number two challenges are in the business right now. Ask, *"If I could help you to overcome the two biggest challenges when recruiting right now, what would those be?"*

Wait for a response...

Once they have given you their two biggest challenges you can ask, *"What are the implications for the business if these challenges continue?"*

Wait for a response...

"What are the implications for you on a personal level if these challenges continue?"

Wait for a response…

"If I could help you to overcome (name of two challenges), I guess you would be open to that?"

Then you present a solution to their problem.

The ultimate recruitment sales agenda

The 19 words you must use at the beginning of every sales meeting that will increase your conversion by 20%!

Picture the scene….

You have arrived at your client's premises (or you've called your client at the agreed time on the phone). You are full of enthusiasm and positive energy. After all, the client has requested your report, they have had emails and a letter from you, and you've spoken to them on the phone and have some idea of what sort of recruitment they will be doing.

You've been shown into his or her office and been offered a drink. You've both exchange pleasantries, now what?

Do you ask for the job order?

Probably not, there is still some work to be done.

You've got to create a favourable *beginning* that gets their attention and puts you in a positive light.

Here are 19 words that you can use in your opening to increase your conversion by 20%.

"I have been thinking about our meeting and have prepared an agenda" - you pass over the agenda - *"is there anything you'd like to add?"*

These words have been specifically chosen to do a number of key things for both you and the client.

First – *"I've been thinking about our meeting…"*

Well, that makes a change, doesn't it? Most of your competitors rarely, if ever, do that. What a great expression to start a meeting with. It will make you look so professional and so different and so in control compared with the other recruiters who call on that client.

The next few words are – *"…and I've prepared an agenda…"*

How many people have you ever met, or, more importantly, how many people has your client met who took the time, trouble and effort to prepare an agenda? Again, this separates you from other recruiters and makes you look professional.

Now you say – *"Is there anything you'd like to add?"*

In order to answer this question what must the client do? They must read the agenda. At this point, slide the AGENDA over to the client, then SHUT UP and WAIT for a response. Simple, isn't it?

Yes - provided you remain quiet having asked the question. Look down and read your copy again - the client will read the agenda and then respond to your question.

Because they've read the agenda you've now opened the files in their mind about the topic in hand, and created a route map for the meeting.

The majority of the responses that the top recruitment/search firms have received over the years to this question (and the majority of the responses reported to me by those who now use agendas) go something like this, *"er, no - that's great!"*

Just think about that for a moment...

You took some time and worked out what you wanted to discuss with the potential client. The way you positioned it means the client has now agreed to YOUR agenda. What would it mean to you and your business if every time you had a meeting with a client they agreed to your agenda?

Here are some of the benefits other recruiters and search firms have reported;

"You definitely separate yourself from the crowd, so are more likely to be remembered."

"There will be very few RECRUITERS who call on your prospects who take the time and the effort to prepare an agenda for that call — so when you do it you really will be different and different in such a positive way that it will make a positive impression on the client right at the start of the meeting."

"It means that you can take control of the meeting and keep to the time that has been allocated for it."

"This will be greatly appreciated by busy prospects — and I've found that prospects are more than happy for me to take the initiative in preparing the agenda."

When I was a search consultant, I would often have great meetings with hiring managers, in particular if they had an interest in sport, as I can listen to and talk about sport all day. We would sit there sometimes for two hours talking business and sport; we would share stories about our families and the world in general. At the end of the meeting the hiring manager would say, *"Terry, the next time I need a search firm I will call you."*

I would smile shake their hand warmly and return to the office full of the joys of spring. My line manager would ask how the meeting went. I would enthusiastically explain that it was a great meeting, we got on well and I would certainly get the next search assignment. That prospect would then go into my sales forecast. A few months later, I would hear on the grapevine that the client who promised me the next assignment had in fact given it to my main competitor.

Have you ever experienced anything like that?

Do you know what to do so it never ever happens again?

To get the ultimate recruitment sales agenda template to increase your recruitment/search sales go to www.recruitmentsalesrecipe.co.uk/inner-circle.

Other ways you communicate (without words)

As I mentioned earlier, meetings can be both in person, or on the phone (or Skype). When the meeting is in person, there are some nonverbal ways that you can communicate with your client that will enhance your relationship. Interpreting your prospect's nonverbal signals and behaviours allows you to read their attitude and better understand their needs.

Projecting the right nonverbal cues yourself can help your prospect feel at ease.

Here are some positive and negative examples of nonverbal cues you should be aware of:

Facial expressions

Bad - wrinkling the nose, furrowing the brow or rolling the eyes.
Good - smiling, raised eyebrows, relaxed mouth.

Eye contact

Bad - avoiding your prospect or looking outside your sales space.
Good - looking back to your prospect's face, and at your products.

Smile

Bad - closed, firm or expressionless mouth.
Good - smiling or relaxed mouth.

Hands

Bad - hands folded to the chest or near the face.
Good - hands moving freely, and relaxed.

Gestures

Bad - closed arms, dismissive hand gestures.
Good - open arms, nodding the head.

Posture

Bad - slouching, shoulders turned away.
Good - standing upright, inclining the body forward, mirroring the prospect's body language.

Position

Bad - moving too close, facing away.
Good - observing personal space, accommodating cultural differences.

Connection

Pay attention to the person you are communicating with to get the connection. Give them eye contact, listen and hang on to their every word.

How to build rapport and influence your prospects with integrity

To build rapport and influence prospects requires some essential ingredients. I'm going to share the secrets that create rapid and effective rapport, so that your prospects like you, trust you and want to buy from you.

The best part of this is that it doesn't matter what industry you're in, or how you pitch your recruitment service – these techniques guarantee vast improvements in your sales skills.

Consider this: a CBS News/New York Times poll asked: *"What percentage of people in general are trustworthy?"*

The answer? 30%. Pretty sceptical, right?

Not necessarily. At the same time, the CBS News/New York Times poll asked a similar group the same question, but with a slight difference. *"What percentage of people you know are trustworthy?"*

The answer? 70%. That's a huge difference.

Which proves my point; when people get to know you and people get to like you, people begin to trust you.

The 9 biggest mistakes made by recruiters/search firms when selling

1. NOT HAVING A WELL DEFINED 'DESIRED OUTCOME'. If you can't describe the objective of your meeting in one sentence, you may be guilty of fuzzy focus.

You'll confuse your listener and that doesn't make the sale. Decide exactly what you want and need to accomplish in this

143

contact. What would be a positive outcome?

For example, an ideal outcome could be getting an agreement to meet up in four weeks, before your prospect decides to engage a recruiter.

2. NO CLEAR STRUCTURE. Make it easy for your prospect to follow what you are saying, whether in a casual conversation or a formal presentation of information and ideas. They'll remember it better, and you will too. Otherwise, you may forget to make a key point. If you waffle or ramble, you lose your listeners. Even for a conversation, mentally outline your objectives.

3. TALKING TOO MUCH. Recruiters often talk too much about themselves and their service, and end up boring the prospect. Remember, the prospect really doesn't care about you or your business, they only care about what's in it for them.

Recruiters can be guilty of making a speech rather than having a conversation. The key to connecting with a prospect is conversation. The secret of client conversation is to ask questions and the quality of client information received depends on the quality of the questions asked.

The bigger secret is waiting for, and listening to, the answers! In fact, a successful encounter early in the sales process should probably involve mostly open-ended questions; the kind that require essay answers rather than just "yes" and "no" ones. Also, don't rush on with pre-programmed questions that pay no attention to the answer you've just received. Learn to listen, even pausing to wait for further comments.

Remember, silence draws people out.

4. NO MEMORABLE STORIES. People rarely remember your exact words. Instead, they remember the mental images your words inspired. Support your key points with vivid, relevant stories. Help them 'make the movie' in their minds by using memorable characters, exciting situations, intriguing dialogue, suspense and humour.

Telling stories about satisfied clients and painting a picture of how the prospect's situation will be improved by using your service is really smart.

5. NO TESTIMONIALS FROM SATISFIED PROSPECTS AND CANDIDATES. There's a limit to how many bold claims you can make about your company results, but there is no limit to the words of praise you use from the mouths of your delighted customers.

Use case histories of your prospects' success stories involving the benefits they received from your service. Choose characters that your prospects can connect with. It helps if the star of your story holds a similar position to your prospect. When you are using testimonials, use them from similar industries and sectors; also, send others via email in your follow up broadcasts.

6. NO EMOTIONAL CONNECTION. The most powerful communication combines both intellectual and emotional connections. As mentioned before, all decisions are made with emotion and justified with logic. That is why you ask about the implication for the decision maker if the problem they mentioned continues.

7. NOT HAVING A COMPELLING USP/GUARANTEE. The USP is a statement or message that explains to your prospect, why they should engage your firm rather than your competitors. (See page 97 for more explanation)

8. NO PAUSES. Few sales presentations have enough pauses. Good music and good communication both contain changes of pace, pauses and full rests. This is when listeners think about important points you've just made. If you rush on at full speed to cram in as much information as possible, chances are you've left your prospects back at the station. Give them enough time to ask a question or even time to think over what has been said. Pauses allow pondering and understanding.

9. NOT HAVING A STRONG OPENING AND CLOSING. Engage your audience immediately with a powerful, relevant opening that includes them.

What is Rapport?

Here's what Wikipedia has to say on the subject:

"Rapport is one of the most important features or characteristics of subconscious communication. It is commonality of perspective: being 'in sync' with, or being 'on the same wavelength' as the person with whom you are speaking to."

From a sales point of view, rapport is the state where your prospect just gets you. More importantly, the feeling is mutual – they sense that you get them, too. This state of mutual 'liking' is so important when it comes to getting the business.

People buy from people they like

From the prospect's point of view, a pitch lacking rapport is so uncomfortable that they may not buy, even if your recruitment service is exactly what they need.

On the other end, if a prospect has huge rapport with a recruiter, and the fees are slightly higher, then they will still buy form that person. Rapport can make or break a deal.

146

Take control of your communication

Amateur recruiters leave rapport up to fate. If they can connect with a prospect, fantastic! If they can't, they try and force the prospect into a decision.

In reality, any recruiter is only 'rapport-compatible' with one or two personality types similar to their own. When they meet prospects with a different psychological make-up, they mysteriously can't seem to create that rapport connection easily. The most common example is when highly extroverted recruiters struggle to connect with highly introverted prospects.

They're unlike one another as personality types, so a rapport isn't present.

So how do you take control of the rapport process and deliberately create a state of connection in your prospect's mind?

People like people who are like them. The secret to establishing rapport is to be more 'like' your prospect. It means having the behavioural flexibility to act similarly to diverse personality types – even ones that are polar opposites from your own.

An infatuated couple sitting in a restaurant is the very best example to demonstrate the rapport phenomenon. Although you might not want to recreate this level of connection with your prospects, studying the psychology of this couple can give you insights into how rapport is created.

Create this scene in your mind's eye...

The couple stare into each other's eyes. They're eating dinner, and as he tells his funny story, she pauses eating. They're facing each other, both leaning forward with their elbows on the table. As she giggles, he chuckles. When she lifts her glass to drink, he does the same. They're matching and mirroring each other's body language every step of the way.

After reading this and becoming aware of it, you'll see this mirroring of body language and behaviour occurring everywhere. It's the physical manifestation of a deeper state of rapport connection.

But here's the true secret...

By deliberately recreating the *symptoms* of rapport, you can recreate the *state of rapport*. When matching and mirroring body language, you can send your prospect an unconscious signal that you are 'just like them', and this subconscious, nonverbal communication is the very essence of building rapport.

We all do this unconsciously. Next time you're in a meeting, watch people taking sips of their water. Pay attention to friends and family as you hang out. When are these people mirroring you? Better question, when are they NOT mirroring you?

Rapport is totally unconscious for most people. By bringing it into our conscious awareness, we can become more skillful at it. We can learn to mirror people even when they're vastly different to us. Doing so increases our ability to connect naturally (and sell to) the variety of psychological types we might encounter.

The power of mirroring doesn't stop at body language, though. In fact, it grows as we apply the principal to other elements of communication. Imagine matching someone's beliefs, or better yet, their values!

With whom do you already have a lot of rapport? Where would having some more be useful? What else could you mirror, besides body language?

Practice, Practice and Practice

Some people are naturals at building rapport, and for others it's a learned skill. But the point is, it can be learned. The most important part is making it feel and sound natural, because prospects can totally sense when rapport-building is just another thing on your checklist. I mean, if you just bond about the weather for 15 seconds, it's pretty obvious what you're doing, and your good intentions are quickly wiped away. Instead, have an earnest conversation.

Once you've gotten good at finding ways to open up the conversation, practice the transition to a business conversation. Remember, even if you forge a strong personal bond with a prospect, they still have business they need to accomplish. If you don't get good at transitioning to the business conversation, you'll reach a point where you're wasting their time.

(Note: If you're truly not good at building rapport, all is not lost ... as long as you're good at earning people's respect, and quickly. It's a common misconception that charm wins you deals, but charm alone does not make a great salesperson. An ideal salesperson can do both — charm people and earn their respect — but ultimately, the ability to help a lead is the most important part of being great at sales.)

There is a gift waiting for you from the kind and extremely generous 'Renegade Recruiter'

Before you go any further, make sure you go to
www.recruitmentsalesrecipe.co.uk/inner-circle
and get the tools, templates and scripts which will enable
you to influence your prospects and candidates effortlessly
and with integrity, so that you can increase
your personal earnings.

This normally sells for £287.00/$465.00 but you can get it
FREE! Simply go to;
www.recruitmentsalesrecipe.co.uk/inner-circle

Part 12: Why You Mustn't Allow Some Prospects To Buy From You

The Law of Supply and Demand

What you are about to discover will contradict everything you have ever heard or perceived about selling. However, it is based on the economic principle of **supply and demand.**

Supply and demand is perhaps one of the most fundamental concepts of economics, and it is the backbone of a market economy. **Demand** refers to how much (quantity) of a service is desired by buyers. The quantity demanded is the amount of your service that your potential prospects are willing to buy at a certain price; the relationship between price and quantity demanded is known as the demand relationship. **Supply** represents how much the market can offer.

The quantity supplied refers to the amount of a certain good producers are willing to supply when receiving a certain price. The correlation between price and how much of the service is supplied to the market is known as the supply relationship. Price, therefore, is a reflection of supply and demand.

In market economy theory, demand and supply theory will allocate resources in the most efficient way possible.

How?

Let us take a closer look at the law of demand and the law of supply.

I appreciate that many recruiters will now be thinking, *"are you crazy, do you have any idea how competitive this business is?"* I appreciate that, but bear with me. The fact is that 20% of recruitment firms have about 80% of the recruitment business.

But consider this, most recruiters are struggling or just doing OK.

Incidentally, for the top 20% recruiters/search firms, success has nothing to do with being the best in the market, or having the best candidates or the best database of prospects. A lot of the success is based on the powerful force of **supply and demand.**

This simple yet powerful concept regulates the price of every recruitment/search service

Once you understand this concept and operate within the laws of **supply and demand**, it will strengthen you on a personal level and bring great returns for your business, because, quite simply, this could transform your relationship with your prospects for the better.

As I mentioned earlier, whenever we share this with recruiters, they will say, *"yeah, but our market is different and our prospects are inundated with calls from recruiters every day, if we don't supply them with the service there are a lot of recruiters who will."* And you are right, there are a lot of recruiters out there who will work with anyone.

You also know that there are recruiters out there who will recruit any position at ridiculously low fixed fees, yet interestingly they do not dominate the recruitment market.

But let's look at the top firms in the world and see what they are doing.

These four companies are the four largest search firms globally:

➲ Korn/Ferry International

➲ Egon Zehnder International

➲ Heidrick & Struggles

➲ Russell Reynolds Associates

All these firms work on a retained basis only, and all of them have minimum salary and minimum fees. Yet these top firms have most of the Search business on a global basis.

Do they offer the best service? -> I don't know, as I have heard varying reports from prospects.

Do they have the best candidates? -> There is little evidence to support that.

Do they care any more about the candidates or the prospects than your firm?

Again, there is no evidence to support that.

However, they do refuse to work with *just anyone.*

If you look at the top recruitment/search firms in the USA:

1. Allegis Group, 7,707, 6.2% IT, industrial

2. Adecco, 4,385, 3.5% industrial, Office/clerical

3. Randstad Holding, 4,147, 3.3% Office/clerical, industrial

4. Manpower Group, 4,016, 3.2% industrial, IT

5. Kelly Services 3,464, 2.8% industrial, Office/clerical

6. Robert Half International, 2,675, 2.2%
    finance/accounting, office/clerical

7. Express Employment Professionals, 2,242, 1.8%
    industrial, office/clerical

Yep, at the time of writing this book, the top 7 firms have 20% of the entire USA market. Is it because they are better than YOU? I very much doubt it.

Some time ago, I got an email from a low fixed fee recruiter. I have a negative opinion of these guys simply because they believe that to get more business means being cheaper than everyone else.

Anyway, he explained that he was keen to grow, and he had remained at around the same turnover for the last two years. He explained that he charged a fixed fee of $2000 per placement. He asked for some advice.

I said it is quite simply:

✓ Be a professional and charge professional fees.

✓ If you must do a fixed fee, as the average salary he recruited at was £50k, make the fixed fee 9k.

✓ Only work within a defined niche and make yourself the expert in that niche.

✓ Stop putting your mobile phone number on all your communications and making yourself available to anyone, anytime.

✓ Work on a retained or exclusive only.

✓ Generate more leads so you can choose who you wish to work with.

Now those tips take guts to implement, in particular when you are sitting there waiting for the phone to ring.

Five months later he rang and said he was now billing £18k per month, every month, rather than £4k, and life was easier. If the client refused to work on a win/win then he would refer that client to his competitors.

But look closely at those figures; he was still doing two placements a month but was generating 12k a month more.

He was working the same amount but earning substantially more than he was before when he was selling on price.

The power of disqualifications

Take-Away selling

Humans are nothing if not perverse; what we want most is what we cannot have, and we are often least appreciative of/interested in that which is easily accessible.

Let me give you an example in my own business.

In my business of coaching recruitment/search firm owners, and as an author of numerous blogs and several books, I am inundated with phone calls and emails from recruitment/search firm owners, all wanting to talk to me or meet with me.

The fact is, I only ever meet existing clients who I am working with on our 'Mastery programme'.

Often, potential prospects will say, *"Terry, I only work with suppliers that I have met."*

And my response is ALWAYS the same, *"If you require us to meet for me to work with you, it is NEVER going to happen, so I suggest you take your business elsewhere."*

Don't get me wrong, I enjoy people's company, however, as one of the world's leading client attraction experts, I am also very busy working with recruitment/search firm owners from around the world who have paid for my time and expertise. It would be impossible for me to do the job that I do if I met every potential client that wanted to meet me.

Each month, I offer seven recruitment firms *'Fast Track To More Placements'* telephone Sessions. This is where I share with a select few the latest client attraction methods - they would have to qualify for a telephone meeting.

Yep, working with me is only for a select few, and I decide who they are.

I believe it is Dan Kennedy who said:

> *"Nobody lines up to seek advice from the wise man at the bottom of the mountain."*

It is my belief and experience that 'Take-Away Selling' should be in every successful recruitment/search firm owner's presentation.

Where you've experienced 'Take-Away Selling'

Every 12 months or so, Apple launches a new phone. Immediately the media will report on the queues at the stores, with prospects sleeping outside in some cases.

That, my friend, is 'Take-Away selling'. Do you not think Apple could manufacture enough phones to meet the demand?

What about Luxury Cars?

Below are the world's three most expensive cars:

1. Lamborghini Veneno Roadster, starting price $4.5M.

2. Bugatti Veyron 16.4 Grand Sport Vitise, starting price $2.5m.

3. Koenigsegg Agera, starting price $1.2m.

Each of the cars above has a waiting list of about *two years*. Do you really think the manufacturers couldn't step up production to reduce the waiting list?

There are 3 types of 'Take-Away selling';

1. Limit the *time* that the service is available for.

2. Limit the *number* of candidates available.

3. Limit the *offer*, of say, the money back guarantee.

When using 'Take-Away Selling' it is imperative that you follow through with your 'Take-Away', otherwise you will lose credibility and integrity.

If during your presentation you explain that due to the competitive nature of the niche that you work in, you will only work with three other companies in that niche, you can then explain that you are talking to their number one competitor and you are currently working with the other main player in that niche. You MUST be honest, if you are not then your potential client will know it and you will never get the business.

Also, you must *give a reason* for the 'Take-Away selling'

Example of 'Take-Away Selling' script.

"Mrs Hiring Manager, during our conversation you indicated 'your number one frustration when recruiting (insert job title) is finding candidates who can do the job'. As one of the leading recruiters in this industry, and with one of the largest databases of candidates, I am sure you can appreciate that this recruitment service is only for a select few. As of today, I have one client place available. I am in conversation with a number of your competitors, so that place will be gone in the next two days. If you are fortunate to be selected, and you wish to see the top candidates in the industry, you will need to let me know in the next 24 hours as once this place has gone, that is it."

One last caveat to implementing 'Take-Away Selling' into your business; you must only work with prospects who *value what you do.*

Let me explain.

The Queen's Diamond Jubilee celebrations, 2012

HRH Queen Elizabeth II is the fifth longest serving British monarch. Only four other kings and queens in British history have reigned for 50 years or more. So it was a momentous occasion to celebrate this special year.

The highlight of the second day of the Diamond Jubilee celebration was the Thames River Pageant, involving at least 1,000 boats. Organisers said that some 1.2 million people packed into central London to enjoy the festivities - despite the bad weather.

The family and I went to London to join in with the celebrations. We had a great time enjoying the pomp and ceremony of the day despite the fact it poured with rain!

After a long day we were wet, cold and hungry and we decided that as a treat we would visit the oldest fish 'n' chip shop in the UK - the world famous *Rock & Sole Plaice* in Convent Garden.

As you know, fish 'n' chip are a traditional English dish and it seemed only appropriate that we stick with British cuisine. As you can imagine, the place was packed. The service was OK, but I thought the meal was fabulous and it certainly hit the spot as far as we were concerned.

We were able to take our time and really enjoy the meal after what had been a very long day. The bill came to just over £100 for 4 of us, which included desserts and coffees, etc.

At the table next to us was another family of 4 who were clearly upset at what they considered to be a lot of money for fish and chips, and they were heard complaining that they normally only pay a fraction of that when they go to their local chip shop.

Now, Convent Garden is a huge tourist area, and there are many places to go and eat, from fine dining to pizza and burger bars, not to mention a few venues where you would be best to wipe your feet on the way out!!!

The interesting thing was, we were quite happy with our meal and did not feel it was appropriate to compare the price we paid with what we would pay at our local fish and chip shop (around £20 for 4 of us).

I also felt that as there was such a large choice of restaurants and bars in the area, it was rather churlish to complain about the price, as they could have chosen to eat anywhere they wanted. If they didn't like the price, then why on earth did they choose to eat there?

It reminded me of the two types of prospects you have to deal with as a recruitment business owner.

First, there is what is called the *'transactional client'* and this type is always looking for the best deal and buys on price and price alone. If another recruitment firm were to offer the service at 0.5% less, this type of client would accept, as they have no loyalty. These types of prospects think short-term and see themselves as the expert. They have no desire for you, as the supplier, to make any profit. Their biggest fear is 'could they get it cheaper somewhere else?'

Interestingly, the transactional client also tends to make more demands on you, your company and your time, as it is all about what they can get from you. When you work with the transactional client it can be frustrating and certainly tiresome. I bet you know the type of client I am talking about, you may even have prospects like that right now.

Then there is the *'relational client'*. This type of client is looking for an expert recruitment firm. They are looking for someone they can trust, someone who will meet all their needs, and they value the relationship. This type of client also realises that if they shopped around they would almost certainly find a cheaper option, but that is not the most important factor for them. Their biggest fear is making the wrong choice. The conversation they have with you is about your service, with less focus on the price.

As a recruitment business owner you have a choice about whom you work with. If you only wish to work with prospects who really appreciate what you do and want to work with you on a 'win win' basis, then that is your choice.

You can chose to implement a marketing plan that generates warm leads for you easily and effortlessly, or you can choose to make endless cold calls, the consequences of which are that you become almost desperate when a potential client indicates some interest, even if that client has no loyalty to you or an appreciation of what you do.

Stop trying to be all things to all people

As I mentioned earlier in Part 5, it's really important to have the niche factor. Here's why; the most successful recruitment/search firms have well defined niche markets. When you create your recruitment/search business to cater for that niche market, you then become the sought after expert within it.

Sure, you can go to the bottom of the pyramid if you really want to TRY and be all things to all people, just don't be fooled into thinking that is the way to create a business that is sustainable. As I mentioned earlier, this seems counter intuitive to conventional selling of recruitment; where there is a pulse then you sell!

So, to wrap this all up, it is impossible for you to be all things to all people. As it is your business, you decide who you want to work with. And you must position yourself with a prospect that way. Explain to the prospect that you are unable to work with everyone and you only work with a select few. Interestingly, the more you 'take it away' from the client, the more they want to work with you.

There is a gift waiting for you from the kind and extremely generous 'Renegade Recruiter'

Before you go any further, make sure you go to
www.recruitmentsalesrecipe.co.uk/inner-circle
and get the tools, templates and scripts which will enable
you to influence your prospects and candidates effortlessly
and with integrity, so that you can increase
your personal earnings.

This normally sells for £287.00/$465.00 but you can get it
FREE! Simply go to;
www.recruitmentsalesrecipe.co.uk/inner-circle

Part 13: Overcoming Objections From Potential Clients

At first glance, this may seem contradictory to the 'Take away selling' that we discussed earlier. To make this absolutely clear, you should not be working with every prospect that has a pulse and indicates they want to work with you.

It is your business, so your rules. You should ONLY work with those prospects *you wish to work with*, and on 'win/win' terms. Anything else is unacceptable. As a recruiter, you put a lot of time and effort into ensuring that your potential prospects and candidates need your services. However, no matter how compelling their need may be, no matter how excellent your service may be, prospects will always raise objections and demand additional information. Consequently, you should welcome objections because once answered, they give you the potential to close the sale.

In selling recruitment/search, one definition of an objection is:

> *'A reason given by the prospective client why they are not ready to buy your recruitment service.'*

Your success as a professional recruiter/search firm will depend on your ability to anticipate and handle a prospect's objections.

No matter how perfect your presentation is, at some stage your prospect may raise an objection and how you handle it will make or break the sales game.

Anticipate objections

Objections can scare new or inexperienced recruiters because they are not sure they can deliver convincing arguments to overcome them. However, professional recruiters have learnt how to take the prospect's objection and turn it around in order to close the sale. As a professional recruiter, you will probably put a lot of time and effort into developing a winning presentation to ensure that your recruitment/search service is needed by the potential prospect. Yet no matter how persuasive your presentation may be, and no matter how convincingly you present your services, there will be objections and doubts.

Here is a recent telephone conversation I had with a recruitment/search firm owner.

"I haven't been successful on the phone," he began. *"I just can't seem to get people interested in seeing me. I'm not a natural sales person, so I guess I don't think quickly enough on my feet. Also, with the current state of the economic climate, I don't suppose any recruiters are doing any business."*

I thought to myself, wow! The struggle is really starting to get inside his head. He's thinking he can't sell because of his personality, and he's drawing unhealthy conclusions about himself as a recruiter.

"I'm beginning to think that selling isn't a competency of mine. Truthfully, I've pretty much lost my confidence at this point, and I'm not sure how to make this business work for me."

WOW! His motivation is almost gone and he's thinking of giving up. This guy is heading for trouble!

In my mind's eye, I could see the heart monitor screen going flat and I could hear it emitting that awful beeeeeeeeeeep...

It's time to get out the paddles and defibrillate this guy!!

Lights, camera, action

As a coach, I have often had prospects tell me, *"I hate scripts, they are so unnatural."*

My response is always the same. Think of your favourite film of all time. What was that film?

Do you remember the emotions that you felt as you watched the film? Did the situation in the film seem real at the time?

Yes?

That was because it was a good script.

All of us use scripts or word patterns in our daily life - it's just that sometimes these scripts are ineffective. According to the experts in communication, most sales objections take place when the recruiter has not answered all the questions in the prospect's mind. That is because there was no plan.

Making sales calls with no plan will work sometimes, it is called LUCK! You don't want to rely on LUCK to make a living.

Overcoming objections is very important for a recruiter. It's important to remember that the client may not always give the actual reason for objecting to the sale.

Sometimes, it's actually the client wanting to know more about the service, so they put forward objections to find out more about it. Even the client may not realise this, so it's up to YOU as the recruiter to put their mind at rest.

Going back to my call with the disillusioned recruiter, we started role-playing a phone call, with me as the prospect. I began drilling him on the following list of objections and he wasn't able to answer a SINGLE ONE of them with ease!

Here are the top objections from prospects regarding why they don't wish to use a recruitment/search firm.

Have you heard any of these recently?

- ➲ We don't use recruiters.

- ➲ Everything's going just fine, thanks!

- ➲ I'm happy with our current supplier.

- ➲ I'm too busy.

- ➲ I'm not interested.

- ➲ I worked with a consultant before who…

- ➲ You are too expensive.

- ➲ Send me your terms, I will get back to you!

"Listen," I told the recruiter, *"your ability to get in front of people has NOTHING whatsoever to do with your personality profile or the economic climate. Also, your competitors are getting business with those potential prospects who said no to you! Your 'lack of confidence' is only a symptom of the real problem. The reason you're having a tough time getting in front of people is because you don't know how to handle objections!"*

When you get on the phone, you've got to introduce yourself as someone who can help them meet their business objectives. Show them some benefits of working with you. From there, they're going to hit you with at least one of the top objections to recruitment. At that point, you've got to effortlessly answer the objection. Ask open-ended questions, and get on with the process of finding their pain!

Here's the good news, you can practise and master the skill of quickly and EFFORTLESSLY overcoming these objections!

Here's the simple *Triple A Formula* for overcoming objections:

1. **AGREE**

2. **ANSWER**

3. **ASK!**

First, *AGREE* with what they're saying. Sounds crazy, doesn't it? The goal is to make them right, to acknowledge their perspective as true for them.

It has been found over the years that when you simply *AGREE* with a prospect's perspective, at least momentarily, it brings down their defensiveness and the conversation becomes much more cordial. Next, you *ANSWER* their question quickly and honestly. Then, you *ASK* them a question to take control of the conversation and focus on finding their pain.

For example: *"Send me over your terms."*

Reply: *"I can understand you wanting to see our terms before you work with us. Assuming that the terms are to your satisfaction, if I could help you overcome your number one challenge when recruiting, what would that be?"*

And off we go into the conversation...

Then close for either a face-to-face or telephone meeting.

Another example: *"Everything is going fine, thanks."*

Reply: *"I appreciate that things are looking good for you at this very moment, but what is the one part of your recruitment process that if you could improve, would mean you had perfection?"*

Wait for a response.

"So I suppose if I could show you a way to achieve that, that would be of interest to you?"

And here is the universal formula that can be used for virtually any objection.

It is the, *"If I can, will you?"*

Let me explain.

Objection – *"You're too expensive."*

Reply: *"I can appreciate you saying that. Tell me, Hiring Manager, if I could show you how our service will exceed your current supplier, I guess you would be open to that, wouldn't you?"*

Then wait for the response...

What is interesting about this technique is that sometimes it simply flushes out the REAL reason why they are not going to work with you.

Objection – *"You're not on our PSL."*

Reply: *"I do understand, Mrs Hiring manager, but if I had a candidate who perfectly matched everything you are looking for, would you consider looking at them?"*

The common sense 'dos' when handling objections

✓ Always maintain a positive attitude and be enthusiastic.

✓ Always remember that objections are a natural and integral part of the sales process and should not be considered personal.

✓ Always maintain good eye contact, even when under pressure.

✓ Always listen attentively to an objection.

✓ Always acknowledge the objection and then express your thoughts.

✓ Always justify your viewpoints with testimonials, documentation and references.

And now, some very important 'don'ts'

✗ Never criticise your competition. That takes the focus off you and your company, and you never want to do that.

✗ Never say anything negative about your organisation.

✗ Never say anything negative about your service.

✗ Never tell the client that they are wrong.

✗ Never argue with a hiring manager.

✗ Never lie to a client. Long-term relationships are built on trust and honesty. It is far better to say, *"I don't know, but I will find out the right answer and get back to you as soon as possible."*

✗ Never be defensive as that is a negative approach to an objection.

✗ Never lose your temper with the client.

✗ Never let an objection go without an answer.

It is worth repeating the *'Chelsea Mindset Mantra'* I mentioned in on page 59.

"Some Will. Some Won't. So What?"

In other words, you will never ever convince all your prospects and candidates, so accept that and move on to the prospects and candidates who WILL be more receptive.

How to become an objection handling master!

When you do this, you will make more placements, earn more money and work fewer hours.

Here's how it works…

Some of my most successful clients do this drill with their team at least once a week. They pair team members up and have them fire objections at one another until they can handle each one flawlessly.

Every successful recruiter I know has become a MASTER of overcoming these objections and SO MUST YOU!

Most recruiters hate scripts. I know when I first entered the search world, I would squirm at the thought of using them. However, I soon realised that unless I could overcome the common objections from prospects and candidates, I would not earn very much.

My manager at that time used to say to me:

"You will either make placements or make excuses, you can't do both".

It's worth remembering that we all use scripts in our communication. Be it with your children, such as: *"Do I make myself clear, young man?"* (One that I used to use every day with my three boys.)

Another script often used by me when frustrated at work is, *"I don't believe it".* You see, scripts are just habits of words that you use.

In any communication, it is imperative that you can put yourself in the shoes of the person you are communicating with. I am yet to meet anyone who enjoys being interrupted with a call. With that in mind, it is important that you always get permission to make your call.

There is a gift waiting for you from the kind and extremely generous 'Renegade Recruiter'

Before you go any further, make sure you go to
www.recruitmentsalesrecipe.co.uk/inner-circle
and get the tools, templates and scripts which will enable
you to influence your prospects and candidates effortlessly
and with integrity, so that you can increase
your personal earnings.

This normally sells for £287.00/$465.00 but you can get it
FREE! Simply go to;
www.recruitmentsalesrecipe.co.uk/inner-circle

Part 14: How to Always Get The Highest Fee For Your Firm, Easily & Effortlessly

Here are some words that you probably hate to hear.

- ➲ *"What's your best price?"*

- ➲ *"That's too expensive."*

- ➲ *"Your competitor is offering the same thing for less...."*

Most consultants hear statements like this every day. That means it is important to learn how to negotiate more effectively.

Did you know there is a strategy that will help you improve your negotiation skills, enhance your confidence and ensure that you earn more money?

Before we get into that, let me share a story with you.

I recently lost my iPhone on holiday, so I went back to my mobile phone provider to get a new one. I was shocked to discover that I was going to be charged nearly £500 for the privilege.

I told them that as a long-standing customer I expected a substantial discount or I would take my business elsewhere.

The sales person smiled and said, *"you can go ahead, Apple don't do discounts"*.

Now there's a thing...

Apple don't do discounts, yet it has 19% of the smartphone market and its phones are 500% more expensive than the cheapest one on the market.

Here's a thought for you. Many experts in the recruitment/search sector believe that there is only one person responsible for bringing down the fees. And that is the recruitment/search business owner.

Think about it!

Your standard fee is, say 33%, and your client says they can get it cheaper.

The consultant then agrees to do it cheaper.

The problem with selling on price alone means that you are always vulnerable to a cheaper price, because there will always be someone willing to do it cheaper.

Here's a thought. What would the industry be like if all consultants refused to discount their fees?

"You charge what you think you're worth."

It's worth thinking about that, simply because there are firms out there that do not discount, regardless of what the client says or promises.

There are firms out there that will not do any work for less than 10% or 15% or 20%. Some of my prospects have minimum fees of £25k, yet there are firms that will work at extremely low fixed fees of less than £900, regardless of the salary.

What is most interesting is that the cheaper firms do not

dominate the market. But if prospects really only bought on price and price alone, then the cheaper firms would rule the roost, surely?

Being able to negotiate as a professional will help you make more placements, earn more money and work fewer hours.

So here are the top tactics to help you negotiate

Start the bargaining process off right!

1. Begin with the end in mind. Firstly, some consultants in a negotiation of any type generally start with a clear idea of what they want, and of course have answers in advance to the main issues involved. Yet for many, that is where the preparation starts and unfortunately ends. The result is that, with no 'Plan B', the only strategy is to use what they may feel is a logical argument to persuade the other party to come round to their point of view. Unfortunately, logic isn't always that persuasive!

It is worth noting that most decisions are made emotionally and justified logically.

Skilled consultants, by contrast, not only determine their objectives and the main issues involved in advance, but they crucially plan how they will persuade the other party to agree to their terms of sale. They do this by identifying the possible bargaining points and any sales objections in advance.

2. Visibly react when the prospect asks for a discount. This is a very old technique, and it works. Reacting to the question of discount implies that at some level you are surprised at such a question. The prospect will react in one of two ways. A) They feel your discomfort and will try to rationalise their reason for asking or B) They will look to offer some sort of concession.

Remember, prospects ask for more than they expect. A seasoned negotiator will always ask for more than they actually want, that is the whole point of negotiating.

No deal is better than a bad deal. Obvious, isn't it? But not so obvious when the deal has been in the sales forecast for months, seems tantalisingly close and a few final concessions might close it. But skilled consultants are clear about their worst position and have a credible fallback. They can recognise a bad deal, and aren't afraid to walk away from it.

3. Ask for Win/Win – Every consultant has to make some sacrifices and give something away in order to reach an effective compromise. The best negotiators realise that being tough throughout the whole negotiation can land both parties in a stalemate. Prepare yourself to give something up before you enter negotiations. Whether you agree to meet certain conditions or give a small discount, your willingness to compromise will show the other person that reaching an amicable resolution is important to you.

One of the most effective scripts I have ever seen was used by a top performing consultant who recruited in medical sales in London. Her opening line when a prospect asked for discount was *"Mr Client, I am happy to negotiate if you wish to negotiate on a win/win basis."* (Wait for a response) If you get a yes, continue, if you get a no, walk away.

Then use your company's risk reversal example.

"If I do something about the fees, I will not be able to offer you the full 100% money back guarantee. Tell me, Mr Prospect, which is more important to you, a lower fee or a 100% money back guarantee".

4. Let the client know the final decision doesn't rest with you. This technique is great for getting exclusives and for getting a decision. Once a negotiation starts, most people want to get it over with as quickly as possible. Let their impatience beat them. One great way of doing this is to let them know that you can't make the final decision and you will need authorisation.

Say something like, *"If I can get this fee authorised by my manager, can we go ahead today on an exclusive for the next 10 working days?"*

5. Get clear about what the client is looking for. One of the biggest mistakes made by consultants is on the final placement fee. Let's say your fee is 20% of a 60K salary, your placement fee will be £12k. If a client asked for a 5% discount on the fee, most consultants interpret that as a 15% placement fee, which would then be £9k on a 60k salary. Well, that is a 25% discount, when in fact a 5% discount would mean charging 19% instead of 20%. So always ask the question, *"Mr Prospect, if I could reduce your placement fee by 5%, can we go ahead today?"*

6. Never be the first person to name a figure. This is an expensive lesson to have to learn, but a good one, particularly when offering contractors or temps.

When you're asked, *"what's your standard hourly rate?"* it can be a high-pressure question, and you might often find yourself blurting out a figure that was lower than the one you really wanted. Simply respond to that question by asking a question. *"What's the budget for this contract?"* Often you will be surprised to discover they're offering a better deal than your standard fee.

7. Never ever make unilateral concessions. Whenever you give something away, get something in return. Always script it in your negotiation *"If I can do this, can we go ahead today?"*

Otherwise, you are inviting the other negotiator to ask you for more.

There are some 'gurus' out there who say you should never ever negotiate on your fees. I don't believe that to be the case. I do believe that it is your business, so your rules, and you can charge whatever you choose to charge. You need to be aware of the implications of being too cheap, as you will always attract price buyers who are never ever any good for you or your business because they have no loyalty whatsoever.

By the same token, should you decide to be the most expensive, that is also your choice. Undoubtedly, you will attract a different type of buyer, and typically you will work less and earn more. And that is no bad thing.

Your fees should be set at whatever reasonable level is agreed upon by both yourself and the prospect, in relation to the work that needs to be done. This means that the prospect will be in agreement that the service will be more than worth the actual investment.

Four questions you must ask EVERY time you get an job order

When you ask these questions, you are guaranteed to work less and earn so much more.

Here are the questions:

Q1. *"Can I ask you a few questions to make sure that we will meet or exceed your recruitment expectations for this assignment? Do you want the top performing ___(insert job title)_____ for this role, or do you just want any candidates that we may have available in our database?"*

Wait for a response

Q2. *"To ensure that you get the top performing* _____, *we are going to go into your competitors organisations and find the very best for you. For us to do that, we are going to need you to share in the process by investing in some shared risk. In this particular instance, that would be £_____."*

(Make the figure you ask for obscure, such as £7215,15.)

If after negotiating, the client will not agree to a retainer...

Q3. *"OK, I understand what you are saying, to make effective use of your time and to be sure that you get the best candidates for you and your company, it would be OK to have this assignment 'exclusively' for the next 10 days, wouldn't it?"*

Wait for a response

Q4. "Again, to make effective use of your time, can you give me the dates and times that you would like to interview these candidates, please?" (Get the specific dates and times from the hiring manager.)

If you don't get positive answers to at least two of these questions, don't work the assignment!

Once everything is agreed then confirm it all in writing.

Can you see the power of these questions?

When you ask those questions, you will work on more retainers, more exclusives and you will manage the entire recruitment process effectively so you increase your personal earnings. And you will be working with clients who have some respect for you and what you do.

There is a gift waiting for you from the kind and extremely generous 'Renegade Recruiter'

Before you go any further, make sure you go to
www.recruitmentsalesrecipe.co.uk/inner-circle
and get the tools, templates and scripts which will enable
you to influence your prospects and candidates effortlessly
and with integrity, so that you can increase
your personal earnings.

This normally sells for £287.00/$465.00 but you can get it
FREE! Simply go to;
www.recruitmentsalesrecipe.co.uk/inner-circle

Part 15: The Critical LAST Step

Once you have done everything else in this book, if you don't do this one thing, you will not get the business on a lot of occasions.

And that is: ask the prospect for the business.

If you asked a hundred Recruiters for their best tips on asking for the business, you would get a hundred different responses.

I'm sure you've heard the 'old school' recruiters talk about the benefits of the 'assumptive', 'the alternative', maybe even the 'Winston Churchill' closes.

The newer breed would claim that a sale is simply the result of the relationship, understanding needs and building rapport with the prospects.

While closing/asking for the business is as varied as the recruitment sales professionals employing them, there are some tried and tested tips to effectively close a sale and get the business.

In my opinion, there is something in all of the above. But before you can expect to close a sale, you must first earn the right to request the business, and you do that by asking the right questions and really understanding what the prospect's challenges are and the implications of those challenges for them.

However, many recruiters and search firm owners never ever ask.

Perhaps it's because they are fearful of the potential rejection by the prospect, or the recruiter doesn't really believe in what they are selling or doesn't have all the information required to sell their services. But it is the recruiter/search person's job to ask the relevant questions in order to establish all of the information needed to get the business.

If all else fails, ask this question: *"What would our company need to do to get the business?"*

Then shut up and listen.

Top tips for asking for the business

Ask for next steps

After every call or completed action item, ask the customer what he or she thinks should be the next steps. If they are unsure, make suggestions of next steps that move you closer to a close.

Have a well-defined goal

Each step that you discuss with a prospect should lead you towards partnering with them. With each prospect interaction, remind yourself of where you want to go and focus your efforts on achieving that process.

Prepare and plan

If you've done your work, it's time for you to prepare and plan for asking for the business. Planning means anticipating any last minute objections and how you will respond to them.

Shut UP!

The golden rule in recruitment sales is simple: after a closing question has been asked, the first person who talks loses.

In other words, if you've earned the right to ask for a sale, ask for the sale then say nothing. Rookie recruiters often talk themselves into and out of a sale.

Ask this question: *"What do we need to do to get started?"*

That question is so simple, yet so effective.

> *"I have always considered myself to be just average talent and what I have is a ridiculous insane obsessiveness for practice and preparation"* ~ Will Smith

There is a gift waiting for you from the kind and extremely generous 'Renegade Recruiter'

Before you go any further, make sure you go to
www.recruitmentsalesrecipe.co.uk/inner-circle
and get the tools, templates and scripts which will enable you to influence your prospects and candidates effortlessly and with integrity, so that you can increase your personal earnings.

This normally sells for £287.00/$465.00 but you can get it
FREE! Simply go to;
www.recruitmentsalesrecipe.co.uk/inner-circle

Conclusion

Two recruitment/search firm owners rented an airplane to get to the very north of Scotland, to embark on some serious hunting.

After a couple of weeks, the pilot returned to take them back to London.

After looking at their hunting trophies he said, *"The plane won't be able to carry more than one reindeer, you will have to leave one of them."*

"But last year the pilot agreed to take on board two reindeer, and they were the same size as these," replied the firm owners.

The pilot thought about it and replied, *"Ok, if it worked last year, then it should work this time too."*

The plane tried to take off with the two firm owners and the two reindeers, but it was not able to reach the required altitude. The plane crashed into the nearest hill. After getting out of the plane wreck, the recruitment/search firm owners looked around.

One of them said to the other, *"Where do you think we are?"*

His pal examined his surroundings and answered, *"I think we are two miles south of the place we crashed the last time."*

OK, it is an old joke, but you get the point.

If what you're doing right now to generate sales is not working, and you keep doing it, you will get the same results.

Some owners and directors of recruitment/search firms can barely tolerate the thought of selling. To others, it is all part of the job.

Zig Ziglar said: "Timid sales people have timid kids."

No doubt you have heard the theory that sales people are born and not made. I agree that some people tend to have a natural aptitude for sales.

Over the years, I have had the pleasure of seeing some of the most successful recruiters in the world sell their services. At times, it has been like watching an artist perform.

And that is the point of this book: if one recruitment person can sell recruitment easily and effortlessly, then maybe, just maybe, it's luck. But the fact is, about 20% of the industry are 'masters', and if that many recruiters can, then it is not luck, it is a skill that can be mastered.

And mastered it should be, because without sales you haven't got a business, and if you think that by having a fancy website and low fees you are going to get knocked over in the stampede as prospects rush to your door to work with you, then you are sadly mistaken.

Whether you like it or not, if you don't sell today you will not be eating tomorrow. Harsh but true....

There is the story of the young recruitment consultant who had just completed her first pitch. The client considers his options and decides to work with an alternative recruiter.

On returning to the office, the owner consoles the young recruiter. The recruiter said, *"Well, I guess you can take a horse to water but you cannot make it drink."*

To which the recruitment business owner responds, *"Your job is not to take them to the water, your job is to make them so thirsty they need to drink at our well".*

And that is the point. When you have implemented what I've shared in this book into your business, you will have clients that want to buy from you, more than you want to sell to them.

And that is just it.

Most people who invest in this book will do nothing with it. Crazy, I know, but sadly true. So if you're the kind of person who buys stuff and does nothing with it, then lets end the relationship now.

'The Persuasion, Influencing and Sales Recipe For Recruitment & Search Firm Owners' is a system, but it doesn't magically run itself. While much of the process can be automated and scripted, if you don't implement it and then keep turning the handle, you won't get the results you want.

So here is what I suggest you do NOW. Set aside a whole day in your diary to lock yourself away somewhere quiet and go through it in detail. Then implement what you have discovered.

As a recruiter, it is your responsibility to help the prospect make the best decision for them. This book shares with you how to build a consultative relationship with your prospect. You now know how to you raise the prospect's awareness about potential problems in their recruitment. Problems are good because they give you an opportunity to show the prospect how your solution can solve them. You now know how to raise the implication of that problem for the prospects, on both a company level and a personal level

You now know how to generate a ton of leads without ever 'cold calling' again. You also have a better understanding of how your childhood may be affecting your sales performance today, and what you can do to stop it.

Now it's up to you to do something about it.

There is a gift waiting for you from the kind and extremely generous 'Renegade Recruiter'

Before you go any further, make sure you go to
www.recruitmentsalesrecipe.co.uk/inner-circle
and get the tools, templates and scripts which will enable
you to influence your prospects and candidates effortlessly
and with integrity, so that you can increase
your personal earnings.

This normally sells for £287.00/$465.00 but you can get it
FREE! Simply go to;
www.recruitmentsalesrecipe.co.uk/inner-circle

One Final Thought...

You are not alone

Someone once said the recruitment/search firm owner is the loneliness guy on the planet, and I cannot disagree.

The progressive recruitment/search firm owner usually has a lot of ideas, thoughts, opinions and beliefs that he/she has to keep to himself and therefore he/she feels isolated and alone out there.

Every day he/she battles the conspiracy of the unmotivated, incompetent and downright ignorant, just to get things done. And that is where drewcoaching comes into its own, providing a wide array of products and services to help *you* make more placements and earn a lot more money.

Drewcoaching is the catalyst of the genuinely *'success minded'* recruitment/search firm owner. And with our help they radically reinvent their business and business lives, multiply their income, and prosper whilst competitors suffer.

They alter their thinking and their methods, but I want to be clear about what we don't have here and what we don't do here. We don't have a simple 'magic pill' you swallow or an 'easy button' you push, and suddenly everything magically is transformed for the better, (no such thing exists!)

*To get outstanding success takes a lot of hard work, if that
puts you off then we are not for you*

With drewcoaching you will discover how to *replace*
commonly used cold calling and marketing, prospecting and
selling methods with <u>effective direct response marketing</u>.

Everybody wants better results, but most are unwilling to
challenge and ultimately set aside what's been holding them
back and dragging them down and dramatically change their
ideas and their client attraction strategies.(If in fact they *have*
any strategy at all.)

*A whole lot of people want change but don't want to
change.*

There is also a fundamental truth you must understand. And
that truth is this; all recruitment/search businesses are the
same, in their fundamental need to efficiently and affordably,
attract the ideal clients and candidates to make sales.

If you are a high achiever who is prepared to roll your selves
up to get outstanding results, then drop me an email at
info@drewcoaching.co.uk.

In the subject please put: *re; your great book on sales*

Interestingly, those emails get my immediate attention!

To get access to the scripts and tools mentioned in the book
go to **www.recruitmentsalesrecipe.co.uk/inner-circle**

Whatever you do, take care, take action and ***be relentless...***

References

Alistair Campbell, author, Winners And How They Succeed

Drew Edwards, author, Magnetic Marketing (For Coaches Trainers And Consultants)

Dan Kennedy, author, No B.S. Sales Success In The New Economy

Jon McCulloch, author, Grow Your Business FAST

Neil Rackham, author, SPIN Selling

Seth Godin, author, Permission Marketing

Peter Thomson, author, Conversation; The Power of Persuasion

Acknowledgements

A special thanks to my wife Sandra, who has put up with me saying, 'I have got to finish this book', on what must have seemed like a daily basis.

Thank you for your patience, love and unconditional support.

Thank you to my oldest son Drew, who is also my business partner, for constantly looking at how we can raise the bar and deliver outstanding results for our clients

Thank you to my two younger boys, Lance and Myles, for just being them and bringing me down to reality sometimes with a thud.

And a massive thank you to Samantha Gallagher who is a HR, recruitment and overall genius who keeps me on the straight and narrow, and whose feedback, though blunt and to the point, is always spot on.

Thank you to Dan Kennedy for all of his No B.S. books, and to Jon McCulloch and Peter Thomson, my mentors

A massive thanks to the recruitment and search firm owners from around the world who have shared with me their secret ingredients for *'The Persuasion, Influencing and Sales Recipe For Recruitment & Search Firm Owners'*

Without them this book would not exist!

Lightning Source UK Ltd.
Milton Keynes UK
UKHW01f1027150618
324266UK00002B/130/P

9 781907 308529